John Greenleaf Whittier

The Prose Works of John Greenleaf Whittier

Volume III

John Greenleaf Whittier

The Prose Works of John Greenleaf Whittier
Volume III

ISBN/EAN: 9783743367586

Manufactured in Europe, USA, Canada, Australia, Japa

Cover: Foto ©Suzi / pixelio.de

Manufactured and distributed by brebook publishing software (www.brebook.com)

John Greenleaf Whittier

The Prose Works of John Greenleaf Whittier

THE HOPE OF ISRAEL

A REVIEW OF THE ARGUMENT
FROM PROPHECY

BY

F. H. WOODS, B.D.

SOMETIME FELLOW AND THEOLOGICAL LECTURER OF
ST JOHN'S COLLEGE, OXFORD

VICAR OF CHALFONT ST PETER

γνώσεσθε τὴν ἀλήθειαν, καὶ
ἡ ἀλήθεια ἐλευθερώσει ὑμᾶς
St John viii. 32

EDINBURGH
T. & T. CLARK, 38 GEORGE STREET
1896

PRINTED BY
TURNBULL AND SPEARS
EDINBURGH

PREFACE

THE chapters of this book are, with very few alterations, the Warburtonian Lectures delivered in Lincoln's Inn Chapel in the years 1890-4. The object, stated generally, which Bishop Warburton had in view in founding the lectureship, was to strengthen that branch of Christian evidences which rests upon the fulfilment of Prophecy. While endeavouring to keep that object in view, I yet felt unable to follow the exact lines suggested by the terms of the endowment. It is obvious that the argument from Prophecy must require modification from time to time, as fresh light is continually thrown on exegesis by modern scholarship and criticism. The great advance which has been made in these last of late years has indeed so largely affected it that in its old form it was already beginning to do more harm than good to the cause of Christian truth, and it clearly needed nothing short of recasting altogether, if it was to meet modern needs. The utmost that this book can claim to be is a step in this direction, or it would be fairer to say, now that so many efforts have been made, directly or indirectly, with a similar purpose, a forwarding of the movement already inaugurated by others. This, at any rate, is my purpose in now publishing these lectures in a book form, in the hope that I may tempt others to work in the same field with more complete results. It is probable that many books will have yet to be written before the argument from prophecy can take the place which it deserves to take among Christian evidences.

The form in which these lectures were originally composed has many drawbacks. (1) Being written at intervals, sometimes of many months, and extending over a period of nearly four years, attention had to be concentrated in each lecture on some special branch or aspect of the question, so as to make it, as far as possible, lead to some definite result and be complete in itself. Such being the case, it was difficult to maintain a continuous and well connected line of reasoning throughout. (2) For the same reason it was necessary, for the purpose of each lecture, to repeat arguments which I had already used, and sometimes to gather up briefly what had been said more fully, in a way which some readers of a continuous work would feel to be tedious. (3) In such a long interval of time it was inevitable that the subject should grow in my mind, as I continued to read and think, and that between the beginning and the end there should be, if not a serious change in my general view of the question, at least some differences in the way in which certain aspects of it presented themselves. (4) New works on the subject of Prophecy, and on other subjects clearly bearing upon it, as especially Biblical criticism and exegesis, have appeared in such numbers since I first began my lectures, that statements then made as comparatively new to English ears, have since become so trite, that very many readers will have already made up their minds to accept or reject them.

Bearing these disadvantages in view, it was my original intention to re-write the whole in a form which I hoped would be at once more complete and more readable. From doing so I was prevented from several causes, and have contented myself with merely correcting a few unnecessary repetitions and the like. I do not, however, altogether regret my change of purpose, for, after all, the very defects which I have mentioned may be in a measure an advantage to those readers who have not the leisure or the wish to read the book continuously. Besides, even now, one is surprised to find how many well-read Englishmen seem ignorant of what may be called the commonplaces of Biblical criticism.

One thing I have made my aim throughout, the rejection of all arguments which, to the best of my judgment, the genuine results of Biblical criticism have rendered unsound. If I have by over-caution in this respect not included arguments which may still be used by scholars with perfect good faith and honesty, I trust that the defect will be forgiven in consideration of my honest intention. But it is certainly wiser to err on this side than on the other. I feel sure that the convincing power of prophecy will eventually prove so strong to those who have learnt to prize the religious beauty of the Prophets, that it will need no doubtful support.

I should add that, by the courtesy of the Editor, the Rev. James Hastings, these lectures were published in 1893-5 in the *Expository Times*, under the title "*Hebrew Prophecy and Modern Criticism.*"

I feel it quite impossible to acknowledge all my obligations to other works, but the reader will readily recognise among others, my indebtedness to Kuenen's *Hexateuch*; the late Professor Robertson Smith's *Prophets of Israel*; Dr Driver's *Isaiah and his Times*; and the works of other well-known critics and commentators, which, when I have *consciously* borrowed from them, are quoted in the margin.

CHALFONT ST PETER VICARAGE,
The Eighteenth Sunday after Trinity, 1896.

CONTENTS

CHAPTER I
INTRODUCTORY 9

CHAPTER II
THE SPIRITUAL AND MORAL TONE OF THE PROPHETS   26

CHAPTER III
THE PREDICTIVE ELEMENT OF PROPHECY: ITS NATURE AND ITS LIMITATIONS . . . 41

CHAPTER IV
METHODS OF INTERPRETING PROPHECY . . . 61

CHAPTER V
THE MATERIAL ELEMENTS OF THE MESSIANIC HOPE . 82

CHAPTER VI
THE RELIGIOUS ASPECT OF THE MESSIANIC HOPE . 101

CHAPTER VII
THE MESSIANIC KING 117

CHAPTER VIII
THE PROPHETIC AND PRIESTLY ASPECTS OF THE MESSIAH   133

CHAPTER IX
THE ATONING VICTIM 151

CHAPTER X
THE FULFILMENT OF PROPHECY IN CHRISTIANITY . 167

CHAPTER XI
PROGRESSIVE CHRISTIANITY THE MOST PERFECT FULFILMENT OF JEWISH PROPHECY . . . 184

CHAPTER XII
THE PRACTICAL VALUE OF PROPHECY AS AN AID TO CHRISTIAN FAITH 198

THE HOPE OF ISRAEL

CHAPTER I

INTRODUCTORY

"Whatsoever things were written aforetime were written for our learning, that through patience and through comfort of the Scriptures we might have hope."—Rom. xv. 4.

IT has often been cast in the teeth of theology that, unlike other sciences, it is not progressive. Whether this is strictly true of what is sometimes called by way of distinction "pure theology," I need not now inquire. It is certainly not true of those auxiliary branches of study, without which the more fundamental facts of religion are in danger, to a thoughtful mind, of becoming barren or unreal. To isolate theology, to shut it up as in a sacred shrine, into which it is irreverent to gaze, is to deprive it of its proper use in raising man's spiritual being. And those who do not know its power soon begin, it may be unconsciously, to doubt its reality. If Christian Apologetics especially are to be of any practical value, they must advance with the age, they must be in harmony, so far as possible, with its spirit.

Now, if asked to characterise the spirit of our time, so far as affects our present contention, we should say generally that it is marked by an increasingly felt need of consistency of thought. We feel that every truth must stand in some sort of relation to every other truth. It is not satisfactory to say that the tendencies of the age are too materialistic, or too irreligious. I doubt very much whether either proposition is truer of this than of many other previous ages. But it cannot be doubted that it is an age of unparalleled mental activity. The rapid succession of new discoveries, the fresh applications of known laws to new inventions, are giving a repeated stimulus to thought and intellectual enterprise. We see one sign of this in the increasing demand for education on all sides. We see another, no less significant, in the changes which are gradually being effected in the character of education. It is becoming less and less the learning by rote of traditional facts, more and more the learning how to think. If the tendencies of the age are to solidarity in one direction, they are no less to individualism and independence of judgment in another.

All this cannot but have its effect on theology. Its apparent difference in its character and its methods from other branches of study exposes it to a double danger. On the one hand, the mind shrinking from the difficulty of throwing itself into a separate sphere of thought may be disposed to abandon theology altogether; on the other hand, it may seek to reduce it to the level of other branches of knowledge. Reverence seems instinctively to recommend the first of these alternatives. The second is more in accord with the spirit of the age. But is there no other alternative? Is it not possible, while treating religion with all the reverence which the sacredness of the subject demands, to regard it as a part, even though the highest part, of that one world of thought and feeling and experience in which each individual moves? In a word, may we not, while retaining the religious spirit, adopt more scientific *methods* in the solution of religious questions and so do away with that isolation of religion which makes it sometimes so unpractical and so unreal? If religion is to be real, it must be in touch with the whole of man's being. It must be a religion which he can think as well as feel. And if so, the methods of theological inquiry cannot be so very unlike the methods of other studies, and to translate the thought of religion into the best thought of his own day will be one of the most important aims of theological effort. Perhaps there never was a time when such efforts were more needed.

The work of the Christian apologist, no less than that of those engaged in other branches of theology, is affected by the currents of modern thought. Formerly it was the aim of the apologist to defend very clearly cut and defined truths against a definite set of hostile opinions. In these days both the method and the spirit of apology are undergoing a radical change. The line which divides settled and fundamental truth from the unknown and the speculative is less clearly and definitely drawn. The apologist is becoming more and more himself an investigator, one who re-examines Christian evidences with the view of discovering how far they are affected by the ascertained discoveries of modern times, what their value still is, what they really prove. Again, those with whom he reasons are not treated as necessarily wilful maligners of God's truth, but as men who hold opinions which *seem* irreconcilable with it. These opinions must therefore also be sifted, to ascertain whether they are true; whether, if true, they are really irreconcilable. Theological controversy is losing its proverbial bitterness without, let us hope, at the same time losing its earnestness. And so it often happens that the apologist and the supposed antagonist find themselves working side by side in the search after truth; and not unfrequently what seemed so hostile to religion proves eventually its ally.

The special argument from prophecy in the defence of Christianity is, as much as any other, undergoing such a change as I have described. In the last century it was very definite and very simple. The fulfilment of predictions made long before proved that those who made them had a supernatural power, and that the religion which they foretold was of God. But the religion which they foretold was evidently Christianity. Therefore Christianity was of God. Prophecy was regarded as the strongest of all supports to Christian truth, because it was an ever-abiding witness to a supernatural revelation. It was stronger even than miracles, because miracles appealed almost entirely to those for and among whom they were wrought; but every fresh fulfilment of a prophecy is as it were a new miracle and a new proof of Christianity. Now let us briefly see whether prophecy still holds or ever could have rightly held this position—at any rate on these grounds—among Christian evidences. In the first place, will any one venture to affirm that fulfilments keep recurring of so clear a character as to convince any one who does not already firmly believe the truth of Christianity? Is it not a notorious fact that believers themselves differ, and always have differed, very widely in their interpretation of a large number of the prophecies most confidently adduced as proofs of predictive power? How are we to make up our minds, *e.g.* whether "the man of sin" is the Pope, or Napoleon, or the Sultan of Turkey, or some other of the numerous persons to whom that expression has been ascribed? And if we cannot, how can we reasonably urge St Paul's description as a proof of a divinely-inspired foreknowledge? If we read almost any work on prophecy of the last century, we cannot help feeling that too great a strain was put upon the supernatural predictive power of the prophets. The objection here urged was really as strong then as now, but it was the unfortunate habit of the controversialists of that age to attempt to strengthen their cause by piling up all that could possibly be urged on their own side. In these days the least suspicion of special pleading prejudices us at once against an argument. We will hardly listen to an advocate for truth, unless we are sure that he has thoroughly mastered the objections which he is refuting, and understands, and can even enter sympathetically into, the difficulties which are felt on the other side. The purpose of the candid and no less earnest apologist is not to prove Christianity by a syllogism, but to convince men of the truth. But to do this with any success, he must be in touch with the best spirit of the age.

Now the spirit of the age is on the whole against the supernatural. This feeling sometimes takes a form definitely hostile to religion; but leaving this out of the question, there are many who feel that the claim which Christianity makes to supernaturalism, so far from being the main ground for believing it to be true, is rather a hindrance to accepting it. The discovery of so much fixed law in nature, that it seems all to be governed by fixed law, has much, of course, to do with this. The common desire to simplify and bring under one mental horizon all that is the object of feeling and thought is, no doubt, another reason for it. A world of nature governed by a stern necessity of law—a spiritual world governed by the immediate decisions of an Almighty Potentate, are two sets of ideas which seem incompatible, or at least difficult to grasp under one view. But besides these, there is to the most earnest thinker the feeling that supernaturalism, as commonly understood, tends to banish God as it were out of the world and out of the human heart; that the supernatural world is apt to become too much a subject merely for pious reflection, or for Sunday devotion, instead of being a thing belonging to our actual life. The realisation of a complete natural world governed by law seems to leave no room within it for a God of supernatural agency and environment. That prophecy should claim to be a voice from a far distant world, proving its claim by miracles of foresight does not therefore commend itself altogether to the mind of the nineteenth century. Hence the argument from prophecy with that of miracles has been dethroned from its place of honour as among the chief of Christian evidences. The apologist of to-day appeals first and foremost to a different kind of evidence altogether. He dwells especially on the intrinsic value of Christian ideas and Christian hopes, and above all of the Christian character, on the inspiration which Christianity has given, and is giving to the nobler forms of Christian duty, and on the way in which it satisfies man's highest needs. I shall hope to shew that, rightly understood, the argument from prophecy really does belong partly to this latter class of evidence, while partly it supplements it.

But there is another cause which in recent times has tended to modify this argument, namely, the revolution which has been gradually going on in the whole character of biblical exegesis. The old method was, first, to assume a certain number of facts about the Bible, and then to study it with this understanding. These facts may be thus summarised:—(1)

The Bible is the Word of God, and therefore absolutely true in all its details. (2) The Bible is God's Word to the individual Christian, and hence a sort of handbook of Christian doctrine and Christian devotion. (3) Connected with this second assumption, and partly the result of it, is the belief that the whole of the Old Testament is pervaded by the New. This is well expressed in the well-known saying of St Augustine, that "The New Testament is latent in the Old, the Old patent in the New."[1] The patriarchs believed in Christ beforehand. Moses instituted a system of sacrifices as symbols of the great sacrifice on the cross. The prophets and psalmists were raised up to foretell the advent of Christ, and the fortunes of the Christian Church. The interpreter of the present day does not necessarily accept or reject any of these assumptions, but, at any rate, he does not allow them to prejudice his study of Scripture. His aim is to read it, as far as possible, without prejudgments of any kind. The modern tendency to regard the supernatural with suspicion has had something to do with this change of method, and the charge, therefore, that this very cause has sometimes created a new prejudice in the mind of the critic is not altogether groundless; but the change grew mainly out of the more accurate study of the Bible itself, and of other branches of knowledge

---

[1] "Quamquam et in vetere [sc. testamento] novum lateat, et in novo vetus pateat." Quæst. in Exodum, lib. ii. quæst. lxxviii. (Ed. Benedict. iii. 445).

pursued in connexion with it. The number of discrepancies in the Bible which were thus revealed seemed increasingly difficult to reconcile with an absolute standard of truth. The studies of geology, natural history, and anthropology, threw more and more doubt upon the scientific accuracy of the Bible. Comparative mythology and ancient history, together with monumental records, seemed to supply another and more simple account of the origin of its early literature, and finally the critical study of classical texts suggested the application of similar methods to biblical books, with a view to ascertain their component parts. This, again, has brought about results of the greatest importance to the Bible student. It has enabled him so to rearrange the literary strata, as to obtain a natural sequence of facts and ideas, and so go far towards recasting the history of Israel.

The very processes which have led to the reconstruction of the history have been shewing us step by step the incredibilities and perplexities of the old. Let us mention a few of these points of difficulty. According to the order of our Bible books and sections as they stand, we have to imagine a people first of all receiving in the wilderness a very simple code of religious and social laws adapted not to a nomad but to a settled mode of life; then after nearly forty years of wandering, before they have had any opportunity of putting these laws into practice, receiving from the same lawgiver a code so profoundly spiritual, that we seem at once translated into the age of the prophets, who lived at the close of the monarchy. We find, moreover, this new code containing just those institutions, just those religious ideas which prevailed, or were most fully developed, at this later period. For example, we read in Ex. xx. 24-26 how the people were commanded to prepare altars of earth or unhewn stone in every place where God should cause His name to be remembered (R.V. margin). How astonishing it is that before any such local sanctuaries could have been dedicated to religious worship, the Israelites should, according to Deut. xii., have been commanded on entering the land to have only one altar and one centre of worship.

Our surprise increases when we find that no attempt is ever made to act upon this most solemn and oft-repeated command of the great Lawgiver, that Samuel does not scruple to offer sacrifices at Mizpah, Ramah, and Gilgal (1 Sam. vii. xiii.); that Elijah not only sacrifices on Mount Carmel, but speaks and acts throughout as though the temple of Jerusalem had no interest for the northern kingdom (1 Kings xviii.). In spite of Solomon's attempt to centralise the worship of Yahweh, we find in the south king after king continuing to sanction the worship at the high places. It was not till the time of Hezekiah at the earliest that any attempt was made to put it down.[1] It is curious to contrast the

---

[1] In the face of 1 Kings xxii. 43, 2 Kings xiv. 4, xv. 4, 35, the statement in 2 Chron. xvii. 6, that Jehoshaphat "took away the high places," must certainly be regarded as an anachronism.

passing notice of Hezekiah's action in this respect with the full description of the far more drastic reforms of Josiah. With Hezekiah it is what any good king might be expected to do; with Josiah it is a religious revolution. It is not the necessary sequence of the restoration of the temple and its services—it has a definite starting-point and cause of its own, the discovery of the Book of the Law in the house of Yahweh. This discovery is a turning-point in the religious history not of Josiah only, but of the nation. The king, when he hears the contents of the book, is terror-struck; for he finds that it contains injunctions which his fathers had never observed, and terrible threats for neglecting them. Reforms are immediately set on foot to carry out these injunctions to the letter. The most sweeping change is made in religious worship, the high places are put down once for all, and the phrase "the place which Yahweh thy God shall choose to place His name there" now receives an obvious significance. Besides all this, we find beginning at this time a contemporary literature, which in tone, in thought, and even in style, bears a striking resemblance to the Book of Deuteronomy. How extremely unlikely is all this if this book was really written by Moses, or in his age. Whatever be its origin, it seems almost certain that the Book of the Law stood in close relation to that of Deuteronomy, and that it was written, at the earliest, not much before the time of Josiah. This is coming to be more and more generally admitted by all commentators, who feel that no particular theory of inspiration should prevent us from openly and honestly examining the books of the Bible.[1]

Very similar difficulties have long been felt about the Levitical laws of Moses, and have, since the days of Graf, been met in a very similar way. The Book of Leviticus and other parts of the Pentateuch suppose an extremely elaborate sacrificial system, of which there is hardly a trace in the whole history as narrated in the Books of Judges, Samuel, and Kings. Indeed these Books contain much which seems absolutely to preclude such a code. The biblical student, for example, who has been accustomed to regard Shiloh as from the first the religious centre for all the tribes, is astonished to find that the writer of the last five chapters of Judges speaks of it as though it were a small, insignificant village, which his readers are not likely to have heard of. He therefore finds it necessary to describe its exact geographical position (Judg. xxi. 12, 19, R.V.) There is little doubt that these chapters *in their present form* are late. Comments like those contained in xviii. 1., xix. 1, xxi. 25 point to a long separation between the writer or compiler and the times which he describes; but it is highly probable, if not almost certain, that he is making use of an older document. So little were the three great feasts prescribed in Exodus (xxiii. 14-17) and Leviticus (xxiii.) kept in Shiloh that we hear only of

---

[1] It is of comparatively little importance whether we regard the Book of the Law as actually identical with Deuteronomy, or an early draft of it, afterwards revised and enlarged or merely the kernel out of which it sprung.

one yearly feast, and that, though certainly described as a feast of Yahweh, resembles far more nearly a country rout than the sacred solemnities of the Feast of Tabernacles.[1] We do certainly find a sanctuary at Shiloh in 1 Sam. i.-iii., but it is clearly not the tabernacle, as, on the ground of Josh. xviii., is often supposed.[2] It is rather a small local temple containing nothing, as far as we are told, beyond " the lamp of God," the ark, and, strange to say, the bed of their youthful guardian (1 Sam. iii. 1, R.V.).[3] Again, just as the Book of Jeremiah has a close connexion with Deuteronomy, so likewise we find a certain harmony of feeling and spirit, in spite of individual differences, between the Levitical parts of the Pentateuch and some of the books which followed or closely preceded the Return from the Captivity, such as Ezekiel, Haggai, Zechariah, Malachi, and the editorial parts of the Books of Chronicles.

What I have already said is sufficient to shew why the new method of biblical study is far more likely to yield satisfactory results than the old. Now it is of obvious importance that we should ascertain in what ways biblical criticism affects our view of the character of prophecy, and its value as a branch of religious evidences. But I must, first, revert once more to a very common objection. It is often stated. that the critical argument is nothing else than a

---

[1] Cf. Judg. xxi. 21-23 with Lev. xxiii. 34-36.
[2] The last half of ii. 22 is a very late interpolation not found even in best MSS. of LXX.
[3] It is assumed that the sacrificial altar was just outside.

petitio principii on a large scale. It begins with the assumption that the supernatural is impossible, and hence seeks to explain the origin and growth of religion on purely natural grounds. To bring the results of criticism, therefore, to bear in any sense on such supernatural facts as prophecy is simply to argue in a faulty circle. But the Christian, it is maintained, stands upon a different ground altogether from the critic, and cannot admit his premises. Now it is certainly true that a Christian cannot deny that the supernatural is possible. To do so would be unphilosophical as well as irreligious. It is also true, as already pointed out, that a certain repugnance to the supernatural, but not necessarily an absolute denial of it, has often influenced critical investigations at the outset. But it cannot be said that a denial of the supernatural is the ground upon which the critical theory mainly or necessarily rests. The main arguments, as certainly in the instances already given, are usually of quite a different kind. The chief reason, for example, why critics maintain the late date of Deuteronomy, or of the last portion of Isaiah, is not that Moses could not have foretold the institution of the king and the prophet, or the final destruction of the high places, or Isaiah the state of things existing in the time of the Captivity; but that it is on other grounds extremely unlikely that they did so in point of fact. These grounds are in the one case the ignorance of Deuteronomy which the historical books seem to imply; in the other, that the chapters in question do not on the face of them foretell, but describe as a present fact, the circumstances which preceded the Return from the Captivity. The Christian who believes not only in the possibility of the supernatural, but in the actual existence of supernatural facts and powers among the Jews of old, may yet maintain, on perfectly logical grounds, the position of the advanced school of biblical criticism.[1] And this is being done by an increasing number of unexceptionally orthodox divines.

Whether the conclusions to which the critical arguments lead, as distinct from the arguments themselves, do not tend to modify our conception of the supernatural element of prophecy is quite another question, which it is most important for us to consider. But another phase of modern exegesis, equally important in its results, must first be touched upon. The whole tendency of literary and historical research has for a long time past been towards the investigation of a writer's works from his own point of view. It was Erasmus who perhaps first attempted consistently to carry out this method in biblical studies. But the religious habit which attempted to find in the Bible alone an absolute standard of personal religious faith and morals, one of the distinguishing features of the Puritanical school, threw back again the more intelligent study of the Bible which Erasmus and his friends had inaugurated. It is needless to say that this

[1] That is, broadly speaking, the view generally connected with the names of Kuenen and Wellhausen, as contrasted with the views of Ewald and the earlier critics.

method has once again come to the front. The Old Testament we now read, not so much with the view of finding out what each writer has to say figuratively or predictively of Christ, as to learn from it the facts of Jewish history, together with the thoughts and feelings, to which each writer in turn gives expression. It is needless to say how much this method has been stimulated and assisted by the help of sources, the very existence of which was never dreamed of a while ago. The consequence is that the study of the Old Testament is prosecuted with an interest and vigour to which there has been no parallel in times past. The critical study of biblical books, and the investigation of monumental remains, have gone hand in hand; and we are now beginning to understand the history of what even sceptics must admit to be one of the most interesting and remarkable peoples of ancient times.

There is no part of the Bible in which these new methods have produced more important results than the books of the prophets. These are no longer regarded as mosaics composed of isolated fragments of Christian teaching clothed in a more or less mystical dress; but the prophets themselves live again and move before our eyes, as men who shared the life of their own time, and understood its thoughts, even while they rose infinitely above them. So there is an increasing tendency to find in them more and more the spiritual guides and the practical advisers who directed the religious impulses and feelings of their own day, less and less the foretellers of a state of things which neither they nor their readers would have at all clearly understood.

To sum up what I have said. The tendency of modern exegesis obviously affects the argument from prophecy in two important respects. (1) It often shews that what were previously considered to be predictions of future events fulfilled within the period of Jewish history were in all probability no predictions at all. (2) It makes it equally clear that what were believed to be simply predictions of a distant future have their most natural explanation in the historical events of the prophets' own time. It is obvious, therefore, that if we accept the results of modern criticism and scholarship, we must approach the subject of prophecy very differently from the way in which it would have been approached in Bishop Warburton's own day. That critical views of the Bible will ultimately win general acceptance, at least in principle, I cannot seriously doubt, and the apologist who wishes to gain the ear of those whose biblical studies are up to date, cannot afford to leave them unconsidered. Truth can never ultimately suffer by looking facts in the face. This at least will be my honest endeavour, and I shall feel that my work has not been altogether thrown away if I can do something, however small, towards shewing that prophecy, under what I venture to call the light of modern criticism, while it gains immensely in its intrinsic value, still holds a very important place among the evidences for the Christian religion.

CHAPTER II

THE SPIRITUAL AND MORAL TONE OF THE PROPHETS

"God, having of old time spoken unto the fathers in the prophets by divers portions and in divers manners, hath at the end of these days spoken unto us in His Son."—HEB. i. 1.

IT is now becoming almost a commonplace among writers upon prophecy that the chief value of the prophets lies in their lofty spiritual and moral character. It is urged that the predictive element bears a smaller proportion in their writings than was once supposed, and from a religious point of view is less important than the spiritual or moral. I suggested in the last chapter that both these elements have their bearing, though in different degrees, on the evidential value of the prophetical books. The fulfilment of predictions is what has been naturally most insisted upon by Christian apologists, and of this I propose to speak hereafter. In the present chapter I hope to shew what argument may be fairly drawn from the general tone and character of the prophetic books.

It requires no very minute study of their writings to see that the prophets participated in, and often directed, the great movements of their times. They were statesmen, social and moral reformers, quite as much as, or even more than, teachers of a recognised code of systematic theology or ethics. For example, we find Isaiah hinting to Ahaz the folly of bribing the Assyrian king, Tiglath-pileser, in order to ward off the temporary evils of the Syro-Ephraimitish war. If we accept the usual interpretation of Isa. vii. 6, he is equally opposed to the unpatriotic treachery of those conspirators who were for setting up a foreign pretender on the throne of David.[1] Later on, in the reign of Hezekiah, he treats with no less bold derision the alliance which king and princes were already making with Egypt, a power who could do nothing more helpful than " sitting still " (xxx. 7). The prophet Jeremiah is equally urgent in his protests against seeking Egyptian aid. But in another respect his policy is essentially different from that of Isaiah. The power of Assyria had by this time succumbed to its ancient vassal Babylonia, which had taken Assyria's place as the rival with Egypt for the empire of the East. We might have expected that Jeremiah, following Isaiah's policy, would have counselled resistance to the heathen Babylonia. But far from it; he insisted repeatedly that the only chance of safety for Israel lay in loyal submission to Babylon; and when Jerusalem was actually being besieged by Nebuchadrezzar's army, counsels without hesitation the unconditional surrender (Jer. xxi. 9, &c.). With equal firmness he afterwards opposes all attempts to resist the Philo-Babylonian

---

[1] The form of the name Tabeel seems to shew that he was of Aramaic origin. See Cheyne, *in loco*.

deputy, Gedaliah, and to go down into Egypt (Jer. xl.-xliv.). It was this political cowardice and want of patriotism, as it seemed, far more than any unpopularity in his religious teaching as such, which so irritated Jeremiah's opponents. (See *e.g.* xxxvii. 11-21).

It is clear from such examples as these that the prophets took a very prominent part in questions of foreign policy. And yet to speak of the prophets as politicians is in a way to mistake their true character. They were not politicians in the sense that Wolsey and Richelieu were politicians. Their political attitude was in all cases the result of religious conviction. Isaiah maintained stoutly that to seek any foreign alliance at all was an irreligious act of distrust and disloyalty to God. It was to refuse the peaceful waters of Shiloah, which, by its very name, typified the safety of the people of God. It was to build on another foundation than the precious corner-stone which God laid in Zion. To seek the help of Egypt was, as he puts it, with characteristic irony, to trust in those who, after all, were only men, not God, and horses which were flesh not spirit, and to refuse to look unto the Holy One of Israel. (See Isa. viii. 6; xxviii. 16; xxxi. 1-3). It may be questioned to what extent the difference of Jeremiah's policy may be explained by a natural difference of temperament, and how far it was due to the altered circumstances of the time. But in any case it took a religious form, and was directly prompted by religious feeling. Jeremiah believed with unflinching certainty that Babylon was God's instrument designed to punish His people, who were now past reform. To resist Babylon, therefore, was to resist the power of God. To attempt to upset their government in Jerusalem was to rebel against God's punishment.

It is equally obvious, and yet equally important to bear in mind, that in matters of moral and social reform the prophets were none the less acting under religious motives. If we extend the word religion so as to include all social and moral duty, this is, of course, a truism. But the prophets were religious in a higher, if also a narrower, sense of the word. The gross immoralities and cruelties of their time were wrong, because they were violations of God's law. The prophets do not, as we might naturally have expected, appeal to an abstract principle of right and wrong, nor even to the law of conscience as St. Paul conceived it, in the Epistle to the Romans for example, but to a recognised Divine standard of right, that which God teaches, the Instruction or Torah.[1] Now modern criticism tends to shew more and more clearly that this Instruction is the religious tradition as taught by the prophets.[2] By this is not meant, of course, as the Rabbinical schools believed, a great collection of oral precepts supplementary to the Pentateuch, and handed down verbatim from the time of

---

[1] The meaning of the word תורה is obscured in our English Bibles by the translation "law."

[2] See Robertson Smith, *Old Testament in Jewish Church*. 2nd ed. p. 299.

Moses. It was rather, it would seem, a revelation of religious duty which had begun not improbably with Moses, and had been developed by the great religious teachers acting under Divine Providence. That such was the opinion in the later days of the monarchy is clear from the well-known words of Deuteronomy xviii. 15, if we accept the late date now usually assigned to that book, "Yahweh thy God will raise up unto thee a prophet from the midst of thee, of thy brethren, like unto me; unto him ye shall hearken." Whatever view we take of the date of Deuteronomy, these words can hardly be referred solely to Christ; for it would have been little consolation to those who lost their teacher in Moses to know that another equally great would arise many centuries after their time. It is now generally admitted that the words must be so understood as to include the whole prophetic order, which did as a fact prepare the way for a Prophet who was far greater than Moses. The passage shews that at the time when this book was written it was believed that the prophets were designed to continue the revelation of religion which had been begun in Moses.

It has often been insisted upon by theological writers, from Bishop Butler downwards, that the prophets lay greater stress on the moral law than on what are known as positive precepts,[1] that is to say, precepts laid down by external even though Divine authority, as especially the ceremonial law of the Jews, and

---

[1] See *e.g.*, Butler's *Analogy*, Pt. ii. ch. 1 (Angus's ed. p. 163 ff.).

claiming obedience only because of that authority. Such a distinction expresses, from our Christian point of view, a very real truth; but it was not felt, as we feel it, by the prophets themselves. The very passage from Hosea (vi. 6) which Butler takes as the keynote of this distinction, "I desire mercy, and not sacrifice," shews clearly the prophet's view of the subject. The superiority of mercy (if that and not rather piety is the true meaning of the Hebrew חסד) over sacrifice lay in the very fact that it was God's will, not, of course, as by an arbitrary decree, but as flowing out of the whole character and being of God. On the other hand, sacrifices were not in the same sense Divine. They were not a distinctive mark of God's people. They were common, at the time when the earlier prophets wrote, to all the nations around; and, as far as can be gathered, there was no very obvious difference between the worship of Yahweh, at least at the several sanctuaries scattered throughout the northern kingdom, and that of the heathen gods. Indeed it is often very difficult to determine with certainty with which of the two the rites condemned by the prophets were connected. For example, a cursory reading of the prophet Hosea might lead us to suppose that the chief object of his prophecies was to condemn heathen worship. But a closer examination makes it evident that the people addressed were, at least in theory, worshippers of Yahweh. What is condemned is the want of reality in the worship, and its association with all forms of ungodliness in the Jewish sense of the word.

"They have not cried unto Me with their heart, but they howl upon their beds; they assemble themselves for corn and wine, they rebel against Me" (vii. 14). Their religious service was at best a mere gathering together to get what they could out of God. And the natural punishment of all this is that God will not accept their sacrifices. "As for the sacrifices of mine offerings, they sacrifice flesh and eat it; but Yahweh accepteth them not: now will He remember their iniquity and visit their sins" (viii. 13). And so Hosea foretells that the sanctuaries, with all their paraphernalia of worship, altars, pillars, and calves, would be swept away (x. 1, 2, 5).

It is sometimes maintained that what Hosea condemns is the worship of the calves, as a distinct cult, and that on the grounds of its being schismatical, or even heathenish. It is quite true that the calf-worship of Bethel, or Beth-Aven as Hosea nicknames it, was his great aversion; but he speaks in very disparaging terms also of other sanctuaries, such as Gilgal (iv. 15) and Shechem (vi. 9), and yet he never objects to them or to Bethel on the ground that they were schismatical.[1] Heathenish, no doubt, he felt them to be, not, however, because false deities were worshipped there, but because Yahweh was worshipped under a degrading symbolism. Even could we suppose that Hosea is attacking the great national schism, there can certainly be no doubt about Isaiah. And

[1] The illusion in iii. 5 is to the monarchical government of David, not to the Temple worship of Jerusalem.

Spiritual and Moral Tone of the Prophets. 33

yet, while speaking unmistakably of the orthodox temple worship of Jerusalem, Isaiah uses language of, if possible, still greater severity. "To what purpose is the multitude of your sacrifices unto ME? saith Yahweh: I am full of the burnt-offerings of rams, and the fat of fed beasts; and I delight not in the blood of bullocks, or of lambs, or of he-goats. When ye come to see My face, who hath required this at your hand, to trample My courts? Bring no more vain oblations; incense is an abomination unto Me; new moon and sabbath, the calling of assemblies,—I cannot away with iniquity and the solemn meeting. Your new moons and your appointed feasts My soul hateth: they are a trouble unto Me; I am weary to bear them. And when ye spread forth your hands, I will hide mine eyes from you: yea, when ye make many prayers, I will not hear: your hands are full of blood" (i. 11-15).

It may be said, and quite justly, that the language of the prophets in such passages is rhetorical, and that they would not have seriously advocated the abolition of sacrifices. But at any rate it is hardly conceivable that the prophets would have spoken so had they believed, as the later Jews believed, that all the details of religious worship had been ordained by Moses under the direct sanction of God. Indeed, there are passages which seem expressly to deny this. In v. 25, 26, Amos says; "Did ye bring unto *Me* sacrifices and offerings in the wilderness forty years, O house of Israel? Yea, ye have borne Siccuth your king and Chiun your images, the star of your god, which ye made to yourselves." Whatever be the meaning of the difficult expressions of this last verse, the passage shews clearly enough that Amos knew nothing of an elaborate system of Tabernacle worship carried on during the forty years of the wanderings. And, as has been frequently pointed out by Kuenen and others, if such a system existed, Jeremiah must have made a very serious historical blunder when he said: "For I spake not unto your fathers, nor commanded them in the day that I brought them out of the land of Egypt, concerning burnt-offerings or sacrifices: but this thing I commanded them, saying, Hearken unto my voice, and I will be your God, and ye shall be My people: and walk ye in all the way that I command you, that it may be well with you."[1]

The essential difference between the Jewish and the heathen religions lay not so much in their manner of religious devotion as in their conception of God. The Jewish conception may not perhaps have been perfectly clear, or even always consistent as an object of thought, but it was intensely spiritual, inspiring, and real. God is now a righteous King, the source of just government, now a loving Father, the pattern of tenderness and affection. "When Israel was a child, then I loved him, and called My son out of Egypt" (Hosea xi. 1). At other times He is the Director of natural forces, the God of Nature, or again (as in

---

[1] Jer. vii. 22, 23; See Kuenen, *Hexateuch*, English Translation, p. 175.

Amos ix. 7), one who orders and disposes of the nations of the world. " Are ye not as the children of the Ethiopians unto Me, O children of Israel, saith Yahweh! Have not I brought up Israel out of the land of Egypt, and the Philistines from Caphtor, and the Syrians from Kir?" Such was the God of the prophets, and for man to be unlike God was an offence against God's holiness. Immorality, therefore, whether it take the form of lust or of an unjust rapacity, or of violence and murder, or any other form, is irreligious and God cannot endure it. This is not the way in which we should generally argue now. We should probably rather say that morality depends ultimately on the sense of right and wrong, and that one great argument for Christianity is that, judged by our moral standard, its conception of God and duty is so high. But the Jew reversed this argument. That these qualities belonged to God needed for him no proof; and they were right and moral in his eyes, just because they belonged to God. Of course we must not suppose that such religious conceptions were universal among the people, or had always been clearly understood. The warnings of the prophets shew only too clearly how irreligious, in the prophet's sense of the word, the people often were. But yet the prophets do not come forward as the teachers of a new religion, but to restore or confirm the old religion of the nation. They can and do frequently appeal to existing religious ideas and feelings, and in doing so they develope these on their logical lines, and so, step by step, the thought of the one omnipotent and just King of all the peoples of the earth takes the place of the narrower conception of a merely local deity, jealous if his nation had anything to do with foreign gods, or if other nations interfered with his own peculiar property.

In a word, there are two important facts to be observed about the religion of the Israelites: (1) that they had far nobler conceptions of God and moral duty than were generally current among any other ancient people; and (2) that it was the prophets who expanded these conceptions, and so impressed them that they have become the common heritage of all highly-civilised races. No one of average intelligence and taste can now read the prophets with the help of the best commentaries without feeling that he has in them a perfect mine of spiritual wealth and beauty. And yet it is a strange thing that, with all our talk about the Englishman's love for the Bible, I do not suppose that by intelligent students one-tenth part of the time and attention is devoted to the Jewish prophets that is freely given to Shakspeare or to Browning.

Let us now see how far what has been said bears upon the evidential value of the prophets (remembering that we are not at present taking into account the fulfilment of predictions). An objector might urge that what has been said hitherto only shews the high literary and religious value of the prophets themselves, but this is no proof of the truth of Christianity. To this it might be replied that, taken by itself, it certainly does not constitute a logical proof. If the Christian apologist of to-day were required, like the apologists of the last century, to prove the truth of Christianity by a syllogism, such evidence might very probably be useless. But in fact it may be employed as part of a very practical proof. If a person were to lay claim to certain supernatural powers or, at any rate, to being a special instrument of Divine Providence, and his life was immoral or his teaching irreligious, we should be certainly justified in regarding him as an impostor. But if, on the other hand, his character and teaching were uniquely pure and spiritual, exercising an exceptionally high and religious influence on others, we should feel it only right to carefully examine his claims. Now it is important to notice that the criterion laid down in Deuteronomy for testing a prophet is not so much his supernatural power of vaticination, as the religious soundness of his teaching (Deut. xiii. 1-3). "If there arise in the midst of thee a prophet, or a dreamer of dreams, and he give thee a sign or a wonder, and the sign or the wonder come to pass, whereof he spake unto thee, saying, Let us go after other gods, which thou hast not known, and let us serve them; thou shalt not hearken unto the words of that prophet, or unto that dreamer of dreams." These words become all the more significant if it is true that Deuteronomy was written in what has been called the golden age of Hebrew prophecy.

What, then, the religious character of the prophets

does for the proof of Christianity is at least this,—to make us listen with reverence to whatever testimony they have to give us. It prejudices us, and rightly prejudices us, in their favour. One of the greatest hindrances to faith, in the last century, was an irreverent spirit; and, though this is much less prevalent in the present day, it is very far from having died out. We cannot read much of the sceptical and atheistic literature of our own time without feeling that even now unbelief is often due far more fundamentally to a want of religious feeling than to any intellectual doubt. To one religiously, though not intellectually deficient, a serious study of the prophets might prove a new and inspiring power leading him to that higher religion which was fulfilled in Jesus Christ. And here I cannot forbear noticing what a very great service the higher criticism of the Old Testament has rendered us. It cannot be doubted that, at any rate until recently, the Old Testament was fast losing its hold on the most thoughtful men of our time. It was horrible to think that the wholesale massacre of the Canaanites could have been a direct command from God; that we should have held up for our admiration the cold-blooded treachery of a Jael; that a man of David's moral character could have been a man after God's own heart; or that God should have concerned Himself in a blood-feud which involved such a tragedy as that of Rizpah, the daughter of Aiah. Such things have repeatedly shocked the moral sense and chilled the most earnest faith, and have too often practically shut up the Old Testament, if not the Bible altogether. But criticism has come in time to save us. It has shewn how God step by step led His people out of a crude state of civilisation into a purer religion and a nobler life. This last we find in the prophets. They stand on that higher level of Jewish theology and Jewish religion which was reached even in the Old Testament. This may be called an exaggeration, and it may be objected, by way of example, that in the case of Hosea we find an immoral action distinctly said to have been commanded by God (Hos. i. 2). But it is almost certain that, rightly understood, Hosea's conduct was no breach of social sanctity, but rather an act of unselfish tenderness, for which he was only too cruelly requited by his unfaithful wife.

But the higher religious tone of the prophets does more than predispose the serious to consider their testimony for Christianity; it is also part of a direct proof which may be summarised thus. The prophets were witnesses to their own generation of a clearer knowledge of God and of a nobler standard of religious duty. At the same time, they claim in both respects to be the mouthpieces of God, declaring His will. If we believe that there is a Source of all good, guiding man through history to a higher life and a more perfect knowledge of Himself, there are the strongest reasons for thinking that this claim is a just one. If so, the religion which they taught was a revelation from God, and is at least relatively true,—relatively, that is, to the capacity of their contemporaries to receive it. This is all that, as Christians, we need desire to prove. For if Christ could say even of the new revelation, "I have yet many things to say unto you, but ye cannot bear them now," we must expect that the earlier revelation would have left something better for men to strive after and learn. The very imperfection, then, of the prophets' teaching, as judged by the more perfect standard of the New Testament, is in reality a strong argument in favour of Christianity. For it shews us that prophecy represents only a stage in the history of a revelation spoken by divers portions and in divers manners, and which only found its completeness in the teaching of the Son of God.

CHAPTER III

THE PREDICTIVE ELEMENT OF PROPHECY: ITS NATURE AND ITS LIMITATIONS

"Surely the Lord Yahweh will do nothing, but He revealeth His secret unto His servants the prophets."—AMOS iii. 7.

THE rejection of the supernatural is a common feature of modern thought. A still commoner thing is to experience a difficulty in drawing a definite line between the natural and the supernatural. This is, after all, only another way of doubting how large a sphere of God's work is properly covered by the word "natural." A discussion of the subject is apt to degenerate into a mere question of words. It is of little importance for us to decide whether prophetic prediction should be called supernatural or not; it is of very great importance that we should form some idea of what prophetic prediction really meant. There was a time when among religious believers such an inquiry would have seemed superfluous. It was assumed almost as a matter of course that prophecy was a fore-writing of history,[1] and hence implied a

---

[1] As *e.g.*, by Butler: "Prophecy is nothing but the history of events before they come to pass," *Analogy*, pt. ii. ch. vii. (Angus's ed. p. 272).

power altogether different in kind, as well as in degree, from any purely human faculty. If the word "supernatural" had a meaning anywhere, it certainly had it in prophecy. But times are changed, and even religious men are seriously asking whether the prophets had any real predictive power at all. We feel therefore bound, before we attempt to draw any argument from prophetic prediction, to ask whether the prophets had this power and, if they had, what were its nature and its limits? This inquiry will form the subject of the present chapter. It will be convenient for the present to limit the discussion to such predictions as are believed to have been fulfilled in events connected with Jewish history.

That the prophets were believed, and *themselves claimed*, to have a predictive power seems capable of easy demonstration.

(1) It is suggested by some of the names of the prophetic office. We cannot, it is true, prove it from the ordinary name נביא. That word, indeed, seems to imply a divine inspiration, but this would not necessarily include an insight into the future. It is otherwise with the almost synonymous words ראה and חזה, both of which are usually rendered in the Authorised Version by "seer." Even these words do not in themselves absolutely imply a predictive faculty. A vision might be a vision of the past, as that of Michaiah (1 Kings xxii. 19-22), or of the present, as that of Isaiah, recorded in ch. vi. But a predictive faculty was evidently thought of in the popular conception of the office, as

we see from the figure of the watchman so frequently applied to the prophet. Just as the watchman has a longer range of view than others, so the prophets are able to look farther than others into coming events. Thus in Isa. xxi. 6-9 the prophetic watchman sees from his watchtower the fall of Babylon, which is evidently depicted as future. In the next prophecy (*ibid.* 11, 12) the watchman foresees the chequered career of Edom. One out of Seir anxiously calls out to him, " Watchman, what of the night ? Watchman, what of the night ? " *i.e.* " How long is it before the dawn of prosperity is to rise upon a night of adversity ? " And the watchman, as though he sees a faint streak of dawn above a dark cloud on the horizon, answers: "The morning cometh, and also the night: if ye will inquire, inquire ye: turn ye, come." As much as to say: "There is to be but a brief period of relaxation followed by renewed adversity, from which there will be no recovery except by conversion." Similarly, from his watchtower, Habakkuk sees the future fate of Jerusalem at the hand of the Chaldeans (ch. ii.). The words of Amos iii. 7, " Surely the Lord Yahweh will do nothing, but He revealeth His secret unto His servants the prophets," suggest the popular conception of a prophet, one who sees the mysteries of God, especially His future dealings with His people.

(2) We may notice the universal belief among both Jews and Christians that the prophetic books were predictive. This belief we may consider to have been exaggerated, and the force of its employment as an

argument for the predictive faculty of the prophets in proportion weakened, through the mystical interpretation of the Allegorists, who delighted in finding predictive mysticism not only in prophecy, but in all Jewish narrative and Jewish ceremonial; but this is hardly sufficient to explain the universal prevalence of the belief. But we need not lay much stress on this argument, for (3) the historical and prophetical books alike make it evident that the prophets themselves claimed to exercise such a power. In what is undoubtedly a very ancient fragment of history (1 Sam. ix.) Saul is represented as going to consult the seer, to know whether he would recover his father's asses. This is on the recommendation of his servant, who says of Samuel that "everything that he saith cometh surely to pass." Elijah and Elisha are sometimes instanced to shew that the original function of the Jewish prophet was not to foretell the future. But we must bear in mind that scarcely anything of their teaching has been preserved. Little as that is, the predictive element is by no means absent. It was the prophecy of the three years' famine that, according to the narrative of Kings, established Elijah's claim to be a prophet. He also foretells the doom of the house of Jezreel for the judicial murder of Naboth (1 Kings xxi. 21-24). Elisha also, among other predictions, foretells the raising of the siege of Samaria by the Syrians (2 Kings vii.). Later on, Jonah is said to have foretold the recovery of the trans-Jordanic territory by Jeroboam II. (2 Kings

xiv. 25). These passages clearly prove that from the first the prophets must have at least claimed the power of prediction. When we come to the literary prophets, predictive utterances become so frequent, that it is hardly necessary to give examples, especially as we have already noticed some, and shall have to speak of others for another purpose.

But we now come to a more difficult question. Were their claims justified by the event? (1) First I may be permitted to repeat an argument in the last chapter, that the high religious and moral tone of the prophets gives us a right to assume that they were not impostors, but honestly believed that they possessed this power.[1] There is nothing in their teaching to suggest that they would have thought it right to do evil that good might come. To this we may add that their dignified self-control, as well as the general respect in which they were held, almost equally preclude the likelihood that they were fanatics.

(2) We have also direct evidence of the fact. But at this point we are at once met by the critical difficulty. We should hardly be wise in laying stress on the fulfilled predictions of Elijah and Elisha, as we should be naturally met with the objection that these are popular stories, and that we cannot vouch for their historic accuracy. Again, we cannot now reasonably maintain that Isaiah foretold, in chs. xl. *ff*, the release from the Babylonish captivity under the auspices of Cyrus. Modern criticism again does not

See p. 37.

allow us to argue from the prophecy of the disobedient prophet against the altar of Bethel, because it is held, with good reason, that that episode reflects the religious tendencies of a later age. In fact, we have to face an awkward dilemma. On the one hand, to accept the order of the Old Testament narratives, etc., as they stand, is to prejudice the question in favour of fulfilled predictions; on the other, to assume that predictions are necessarily " prophecies after the event," is to allow preconceptions against prediction to unduly influence our criticism.

The difficulty is a serious one, but not so great in reality as might have been expected. Critical conclusions have not generally been made to depend chiefly on such objections to prophecy, and in many cases we may feel bound to accept them on other grounds, however strongly we recognise the fact of prophetic knowledge; *e.g.* the relegation of Isa. xl.-lxvi. to the epoch of the Babylonish captivity depends,—as I pointed out in ch. i.[1]—not on the impossibility of such events being predicted so long before, but partly on differences of style, and still more on the fact that the state of things in the foreground of the prophecy is described not as future, but as present. The real objection to Isaiah's authorship from the mention of Cyrus in chs. xliv. xlv. is not so much that Isaiah *could not* have foretold his name, as that the author of this later prophecy *does not* on the face of it speak of him as a future person, but as one

[1] See p. 22.

already well known to his readers. Objections of a somewhat similar kind are urged, but with less force, with reference to the prophecy against Babylon in Isa. xiii. — xiv. 23. The style and method of treatment in this passage are different from those of Isaiah, and moreover, would have been hardly intelligible to his contemporaries. Babylon in Isaiah's time was a small kingdom more or less dependent on Assyria, anything but the mighty power that "ruled the nations in anger," as it is here described (ch. xiv. 6). It is difficult, moreover, to conceive a sufficient purpose for the prophecy, had it been written in Isaiah's day.

In fact, it is now becoming a recognised canon of criticism that a prophecy must have some intelligible relation to the events of the prophet's time. This tends, of course, to limit the range of prophecy, and bring the time of its fulfilment nearer to the writer's own day; but not in all cases so much so as might have been supposed. For example, any prophecy against Babylon is in itself likely to have been written at a time when Babylon, and not Assyria, was the ruling power in the East, and therefore is probably the work of a later prophet than Isaiah. But we cannot make this alone an absolute criterion of date, for such prophecies would have been intelligible enough at the time when the Babylonian adventurer Merodach-Baladan was seeking an alliance with Hezekiah against Assyria. Hence many critics, while they deny to Isaiah the authorship of the prophecy in chs.

xiii.-xiv. 23 for the reasons already given, yet believe him to be the author of the prophecy against Babylon in ch. xxi. (1-10). This latter prophecy represents Babylon as a city in whose fate the prophet feels a keen sympathetic interest. It is argued that such feelings would be unnatural if it were written at a time when Babylon was Israel's great oppressor.

We may willingly accept this canon of criticism, and do full justice to indications of date arising from differences of style and treatment, and yet find unmistakeable instances of fulfilled predictions. The Book of Amos is particularly instructive in this respect, because it affords clear indications of its date. We learn from ch. vii. 10 that he was a contemporary of Jeroboam II. He prophesied, therefore, if not so long before as the biblical chronology would have led us to suppose, at least some thirty years before the destruction of Samaria.[1] And yet he foretells unmistakably both the overthrow of Jeroboam and the captivity of Israel. "Therefore will I cause you to go into captivity beyond Damascus, saith Yahweh, whose name is the God of hosts" (ch. v. 27). "For thus Amos saith, Jeroboam shall die by the sword, and Israel shall surely be led away captive out of his land" (ch. vii. 11). "Behold, the eyes of the Lord Yahweh are upon the sinful kingdom, and I will destroy it from off the face of the earth" (ch. ix. 8). Isaiah again foretells the horrors of the Assyrian invasion at a time when the danger of the Syro-Ephraimitish campaign was tempting Ahaz

---

[1] See Robertson Smith, *Prophets of Israel*, p. 151.

to make a secret alliance with the Assyrian monarch, Tiglath-pileser (ch. vii.). This (B.C. 734) was twenty-three years before the supposed invasion of Judah by Sargon (B.C. 711), and thirty-three years before the far more disastrous campaign of Sennacherib (B.C. 701). When that campaign was actually in progress, Isaiah had the boldness frequently to comfort the people with the assurance that it would end in a sudden and complete collapse. We have a typical example of this in ch. x. 24 and following:—" Therefore, saith the Lord, Yahweh of hosts, O my people that dwellest in Zion, be not afraid of the Assyrian: though he smite thee with the rod, and lift up his staff against thee, after the manner of Egypt. For yet a very little while, and the indignation shall be accomplished, and mine anger in their destruction. And Yahweh of hosts shall stir up against him a scourge, as in the slaughter of Midian at the rock of Oreb: and his rod shall be over the sea, and he shall lift it up after the manner of Egypt. And it shall come to pass in that day, that his burden shall depart from off thy shoulder, and his yoke from off thy neck, and the yoke shall be destroyed by reason of fatness." In the following verses he describes in graphic detail the march of the Assyrians, and the terror that they would inspire at every stage of their progress, and finally repeats with majestic dignity their final overthrow. " Behold, the Lord, Yahweh of hosts, shall lop the boughs with terror, and the high ones of stature shall be hewn down, and the lofty shall be brought low. And he shall cut down the thickets of the forest with iron, and Lebanon shall fall by a mighty one" (33, 34).

Of course it is always possible for captious critics to say that such prophecies are the inventions of a later date; but if we approach the subject without prejudice, we must admit that such an hypothesis is extremely improbable. Their very indefiniteness is a strong argument in their favour. A later writer than Amos or Isaiah putting a prophecy into their mouths would have made it tally more in detail with the event. He would have expressly mentioned, we may feel sure, the power by which God's justice on the northern kingdom would be vindicated, if not the name of the king. He certainly would not have represented Isaiah as describing a route which the Assyrians never took.[1] And the same objection applies if we suppose that in such cases the prophet himself composed after the event what he wished to pass for a prediction. Such examples of the obvious fulfilment of predictions are important, because of their bearing on prophecies of which the date is less certain. They make it probable that when a prophet speaks in language obviously meant to foretell a future event, which actually took place, he is really relating words uttered before the event, not a supposititious prophecy composed after it.

But we must now speak of the nature and limits of prophetic foresight. First, its limits. (1) Prophecy clearly neither was, nor was intended to be, a fore-

[1] As in ch. x. 28-32.

writing of future events at all analogous to the historical narration of past events. The prophets did not write to satisfy a morbid curiosity about the future, nor yet to establish by fulfilled predictions their claim to divine power. They do not boast in the spirit of Zadkiel's Almanac that what they have foretold has come to pass,[1] and that, therefore, they are to be believed in the future. They had too much confidence in their divine mission to doubt their power, or to expect others to doubt it. They very frequently do not give the details of future events. Such events have their interest, not so much in being future, as in being instances of God's judgment on sin, or His goodness towards His people. The details when given are often the mere dress in which the prediction is clothed. Take, for example, the graphic description of the future desolation of Babylon (Isa. xiii. 20-22): "It shall never be inhabited, neither shall it be dwelt in from generation to generation; neither shall the Arabian pitch tent there; neither shall shepherds make their flocks to lie down there. But wild beasts of the desert shall lie there; and their houses shall be full of doleful creatures; and ostriches shall dwell there, and satyrs shall dance there. And wolves shall cry in their castles, and jackals in the pleasant palaces: and her time is near to come, and her days shall not

---

[1] Such passages as Isa. xli. 21, 22, xlii. 9 are no exceptions. The point here is not the glorification of the prophet, who does not refer to his own predictions, but of God, who has the power of determining, and therefore foreknowing the future, in contrast to the idols, who can do neither this nor anything else.

be prolonged." We cannot but feel that to press many of these details would be to rob this prophecy of its poetry. Again, in the prophecy of the Assyrian collapse (ch. x.), already described, an ideal line of march is probably added to give a realistic colour to the whole scene; and we are no more compelled to take this literally than the figure of the Assyrian tree with its branches lopped off, which immediately follows (33).

(2) Even where details seem literally intended, they were sometimes not fulfilled. In the prophecy against Babylon just quoted, a far more complete destruction was evidently contemplated than ever took place. Again, the city of Damascus, though taken by Tiglath-pileser, did not, as far as we can tell, become a ruinous heap, nor cease from being a city, as foretold in Isa. xvii. 1. Nor does it appear to have ever done so. It is again threatened with disaster in Jer. xlix. 24-27, and the reference in that prophecy to the "palaces of Ben-hadad" proves that it is no newly-built city which is spoken of. It afterwards became a flourishing commercial city, and has remained so, more or less continuously, to the present day. Tyre did not, as we should have expected from "the burden of Tyre" in Isa. xxiii., fall and then recover itself after seventy years and become a great commercial power converted to Yahweh. At any rate, no such fulfilment of Isaiah's prophecy has been made out so as to give general satisfaction to those who have searched for it.

(3) Again, we find limitations of prophetic fore-

sight as to the time and manner in which prophecies were to be fulfilled. The Captivity of the North was not, as Amos certainly seems to have contemplated, (vii. 11), connected with the death of Jeroboam, but took place nearly thirty years after. The Assyrians did not, as required by the most probable explanation of Isa. xxiii. 13, take Tyre, though Shalmaneser besieged it for five years, nor yet apparently the Chaldeans, as required by another interpretation of the verse, though Nebuchadrezzar is said to have besieged it for thirteen years (see Jos. Ant. xi. 1; Ezek. xxix. 17, 18); but it was first taken by Alexander the Great, and only eventually destroyed by the Saracens in 1291.[1]

(4) It should be also noticed that the prophets sometimes modify their previous statements about future events. Amos, in ch. v. 2, sees no hope for Israel. "The virgin of Israel is fallen; she shall no more rise; she is cast down upon her land; there is none to raise her up." Later on, in ch. ix. 8, after saying that the sinful kingdom will be destroyed from off the face of the earth, he adds, "saving that I will not utterly destroy the house of Jacob." It may be said, and has often been said, that all prophecies contain an implied condition. But this is, in fact, the admission of a very real modification of their absolute accuracy. It would probably be truer to say in such a case as this that the prophet first foretells the judgment as absolutely as he in fact sees it; and then afterwards softens it as he sees some hope for the more faithful remnant.

See Delitzsch *in loco*.

We have now to deal with the further question: What is the nature of prophetic foresight? Is the predictive power capable of psychological analysis? Up to a certain point it surely must be so. On the one hand, we know that a prophet was possessed of a real religious conviction. He felt certain that he was called by God to protest against wrong, whether in morals or in religion, and to assert God's righteousness. He believed that what he said was a word of God, and not merely the utterance of his own thoughts and ideas. But, on the other hand, we cannot help recognising in his predictions a human element as well. For (1), as we have already shewn, there was an element of human anticipation which was not always realised.

But (2) besides this, there was undoubtedly an element of imagination. The prophets are not content with a general declaration of God's judgments and mercies, or a general statement of the direction in which they will be manifested; but besides these, they give descriptions of future events. These are sometimes in the form of visions, as in the last chapter of Amos and in the earlier part of Zechariah, but more frequently are expressed in the language of poetic symbolism. But in either case they give the impression of being the portrayal of pictures present in the prophet's own mind. But how did these pictures arise? Were they, so to speak, written in the prophet's mind by the finger of God, or were they the creation of the prophet's own imaginative power? In other words, is this prophetic faculty to be identified with what the late Professor Mozley called the passive, or the active, imagination?[1] But was Mozley right in regarding the passive imagination as a sign of mental weakness? It does not appear to be necessarily so. So-called thought-readers are not weak-minded or weak-willed men. They shew a peculiar power by the very fact that they are able, when they so desire, to divest themselves of their own intention and will, and to allow themselves to be guided by the intention and will of others. So with the mind. The power to make the mind a blank in order to receive impressions is a highly-developed phase of that faculty which we commonly call receptivity. And every view of inspiration to a certain extent admits this power, and indeed necessitates it, unless inspired men are to be reduced to mere machines.

But does such a power alone explain the facts of prophetic imagination? We can hardly think so. For we find the same sort of variety in the forms which

[1] The passage is well worth quoting in connexion with the present discussion: "When the imagination acts by energy from within, when it enables us to see the force and extent of some truth, to grasp a condition of things external to ourselves, to understand the feelings and the wants of others, to admire nature, to sympathise with man; or when it aids in the work of combination, construction, invention, in thus *actively* imparting meaning and life to facts, imagination is a noble and effective instrument, if indeed we may not call it a part, of reason. But when the imagination exaggerates an impression by passively submitting and surrendering itself to it, when it gives way to the mere force of attraction, and instead of grasping something else, is itself grasped and mastered by some dominant idea—it is then not a power, but a failing and a weakness of nature. We may call these respectively active and passive imagination." Lectures on Miracles iii. (p. 53, 3rd ed.).

the imagination takes in different prophets, as we find in different poets. If we were to say that the imagination was quick and vivid in Isaiah, subtle in Hosea, mysterious or symbolical in Jeremiah, every one would feel that such was an attempt, however imperfect, to express concisely a difference which really exists. In other words, the imagination takes a form which is influenced by the personal character of the prophet. The most obvious difference between a Jewish prophet and a poet is that while the one boldly claimed divine inspiration, and his claim was admitted by his contemporaries, a poet does not seriously make the claim, and would not be listened to if he did. But it does not follow from this either that poets have had no real inspiration, or that the prophets had no power of creative imagination. The difference seems to be this, that the prophet consciously realised the divine source of his utterances, but did not to the same extent realise the working of his own imagination; poets do realise the working of their imagination, but do not always realise the nature of the spiritual forces which, to a certain extent, control them.

Sometimes, no doubt, the prophets consciously clothed their prediction in a poetic dress; but in most cases they probably did no more than describe what they felt and saw, without making any effort to distinguish the foretold fact from its poetic adjunct, the divine foreknowledge from the poetic imagination or the human speculation. Indeed, sometimes they positively refer the effects of poetic imagination to a divine source. In Isa. xxxiv. 14, 15, the description of the wild animals establishing themselves in the desolate cities of Edom is obviously the language of poetry. It is, moreover, so closely parallel to the similar description of Babylon in ch. xiii. 21, 22, which we have already quoted, that the two cannot be independent, and both appear to belong to the period of the Babylonian captivity, and are very possibly by the same prophet. Yet in this prophecy against Edom the prophet enhances the realism of his description by saying that when it should be fulfilled, people were to look at the prophecy in the "Book of Yahweh," and see how exactly it tallied with the event. Every one of the animals would be found there, even the evil spirits, which, according to Babylonian mythology, inhabited desolate regions. "Seek ye out of the Book of Yahweh, and read: no one of these shall be missing, none shall want her mate: for my mouth it hath commanded, and His spirit it hath gathered them. And He hath cast the lot for them, and His hand hath divided it unto them by line: they shall possess it for ever, from generation to generation shall they dwell therein." If this description of the wild animals is repeated from an earlier prophecy, how strange to speak of it as in all its details (for its details are what the prophet insists upon) as a special revelation from Yahweh! If it was itself the earlier prophecy of the two, how strange to repeat with reference to Babylon exactly these details belonging so peculiarly to the fate of Edom! If these details are purely poetical, there is no difficulty in the repetition; but the assertion at the end of this prophecy of Edom compels us to say that the prophet evidently sees before him the literal fulfilment of his words.

But are we certain that there was a divine element in prophecy at all, except of course in the sense that all human faculty is originally divine, and that God by general laws directs human faculties for higher ends? Some critics have resolved the predictive power into a mere human sagacity. Thus the late Professor Robertson Smith, to whom the student of the Jewish prophets is so deeply indebted, in speaking of the prediction by Amos of the northern captivity, writes as follows:—" The danger . . . was visible to the most ordinary political insight, and what requires explanation is not so much that Amos was aware of it, as that the rulers and people of Israel were so utterly blind to the impending doom." [1] But after making full allowance for the already existing encroachments by Assyria, which recently discovered monuments have brought to light, is it not accrediting the herdman of Tekoa too much with that sort of wisdom which is so rare before, and so common after, the event? It is true enough that Amos connects the impending danger with the moral degradation of the people. But the question is whether he realised that this was to act as a natural cause. Was not most obviously his feeling rather that such wickedness was calling for divine vengeance? If we are wrong in reading into

[1] *Prophets of Israel*, p. 131.

the prophets the mystic symbolism of the Cabbala, we are equally wrong in reading out of them their essentially religious character, religious, I mean, as distinct from merely moral. A sagacious politician in the reign of Ahaz might have foreseen that to make an alliance with Assyria was to play a dangerous game. Isaiah saw in it not so much folly, as a wicked apostasy from God, which deserved to end in national ruin. Whatever modifications, then, we have to make in our view of the sources of prophetic foresight, we seem bound to make them not so much in favour of a purely human sagacity (though the prophets were certainly no fools) as of a religious instinct. And this religious instinct, we cannot but believe, was divinely inspired and divinely directed.

To sum up, the position of the prophets seems to have been something of this kind: They were men endowed with a very strongly-developed religious instinct. They felt within them a religious impulse which they were confident was from God. They regarded themselves as His agents to denounce wrong, because it was contrary to God's character and to God's will, and to announce God's judgments on wrong, and His goodness to those who proved themselves worthy of His love. This religious impulse was usually combined with a strong creative imagination which shewed itself in many ways; sometimes by their seeing a deep spiritual and religious meaning in dreams and even ordinary events of life, which were thus allegorised and made sources of religious lessons. To Hosea, for example, as the late Professor Robertson Smith has shewn us, his whole domestic life was an allegory of the religious fortunes of God's people. The announcement of God's judgments and goodness directed their minds to the future in which God's ways would be justified. This combined with natural clear-sightedness produced those often vivid pictures of the future, which though not fulfilled in all the details, which their vivid imagination painted, nor quite as they themselves seem to have expected, were yet fulfilled in their main features, and point to a very remarkable, if we ought not to say supernatural, power of foresight, such a foresight as to us justifies their own claim to inspiration.

I fear some may think that this is a low estimate of prophetic prediction, and I think that possibly my desire to do justice to criticism may have led me to underrate this power. But it would be well to remember that the higher the claim which we make for prophetic fulfilments, the more serious the danger to the cause of truth if they fail the test of honest historical investigation. Christian apologists should be above all suspicion of tampering with witnesses. The more unnatural the strain we put upon the argument from prophetic predictions, the more are we in danger of losing sight of the infinitely more important argument from the moral and religious character of the Christian faith.

CHAPTER IV

METHODS OF INTERPRETING PROPHECY

"Ye shall know the truth, and the truth shall make you free."—JOHN viii. 32.

HITHERTO I have made two things my special aim. The first was to lay stress on the intrinsic merit of the prophetical books not merely as beautiful literary compositions, but as moulding the religious ideas and character of the Jewish people. In the second place I endeavoured to show, that while the prophetic faculty claims and proves itself to be divine, it cannot be regarded as absolutely infallible; that, as a fact, the details of prophecy were not always fulfilled at the time, or in the manner, which the prophets themselves evidently anticipated. In arguing this I naturally confined myself to prophecies concerned with well-known historical events, such as the Great Captivity and the fall of Babylon. If we are bound by the evidence to make these admissions in the historical prophecies, surely we should be prepared to make them in those which presumably look beyond the prophet's immediate horizon. It is with these that the apologist has necessarily most to do, and they must engage our attention in this and the following chapters.

With some reluctance, following the common practice of writers on prophecy, I shall call such prophecies Messianic. For, try as we will, it seems almost impossible to find a name for them which does not seem to prejudge, in one or other direction, the very questions which we have to consider. The term, if strictly applied, is also too narrow, as I shall naturally wish to speak of many prophecies in which there is no mention of a Messiah, and no reason to suppose that the idea of a personal Messiah is latent in the prophet's mind. It is necessary therefore to premise that by Messianic prophecies I mean especially, but not exclusively, those which produced among the Jews that unique hope of national glory and greatness usually associated in their view with an anointed prince. The expression will also of necessity include prophecies which we should now call eschatological, for these are in fact closely connected with the Messianic hope.

That such a hope existed among the Jews needs no elaborate proof; it not only shews itself in the great bulk of Jewish literature of all ages, but the fact that it took a different form among Jews from that current among Christians makes it clear that the one did not derive it from the other. Indeed it cannot reasonably be doubted, that of the two the Jewish conception of the Messiah springs more naturally and directly out of the Old Testament prophecies.

But how are these Messianic prophecies connected with what, again for want of a better name, I shall call the historical? By the latter term I mean prophecies connected with ordinary historical events. We can hardly over-estimate the importance of this question; for on our answer depends our whole method of treating prophecy. As is usually the case, we find among expositors two diametrically opposite tendencies, each influenced, it can hardly be doubted, by a separate theological bias, and depending upon distinctly different principles of interpretation. The first is to find Christ everywhere in the Old Testament, especially in the prophets; the other, to find Him nowhere.

The principle which underlies the first is to take Christ and Christianity as the starting-point, and to search for predictions of these scattered about in the pages of the prophets and other books of the Old Testament. The historical allusions appear at most as the mere setting for such predictions, and as having no real organic connexion with them. Very frequently they have been regarded as bearing themselves a typical reference to Christ and Christianity. Thus in the burden of Moab, Isa. xv. and xvi., and in the prophecy of the judgment on Edom, Isa. lxiii. 1-6, these two powers are referred in the headings of the chapters as they stand in our ordinary English Bibles —the one implicitly, the other explicitly—to the enemies of Christ.

This symbolical interpretation of prophecy has taken two forms, which cannot always be clearly distinguished. In the first, the historical sense is completely ignored or, perhaps it would be fairer to say, is not practically realised, as when, with the Fathers, Lucifer and Leviathan were often regarded merely as names of Satan. Still more singular is the application of the latter term by Rufinus to our Lord's body partaken of in the Holy Eucharist.[1] The passage is worth quoting as a remarkable specimen of quaintness and extravagance:—"*Sicut ergo hamum esca contectum si piscis rapiat, non modo escam ab hamo non removet, sed et ipse de profundo, esca aliis futurus, educitur, ita et is qui habebat mortis imperium rapuit quidem in morte corpus Jesu, non sentiens in eo hamum divinitatis inclusum; sed ubi devoravit, hæsit ipse continuo, et diruptis inferni claustris, velut de profundo extractus trahitur ut esca cæteris fiat. Quod ita futurum sub hac eadem figura Ezechiel dudum Propheta signaverat, dicens, Et extraham te in hamo meo, et extendam te super terram: campi implebuntur de te, et constituam super te omnes volucres cæli, et saturabo ex te omnes bestias terræ.[2] Sed et Propheta David dicit. Tu confregisti capita draconis magni, dedisti eum in escam populis Æthiopum.[3] Et Job de eodem mysterio similiter protestatur; ait enim, ex persona Domini loquentis ad se. Aut adduces draconem in hamo, et pones capistrum circa nares ejus?*"[4] Similarly the same writer[5] explains Hos. x. 6, in which that prophet says that the idol calf of Bethel would be sent as a present to king Jareb, as a " presignification " of Christ sent by Pilate to king Herod! This inter-

---

[1] Ruf. in *Symb. Apost.* 16.
[2] Ezek. xxix. 4.   [3] Ps. lxxiv. 14.   [4] Job xli. 1.   [5] *Ibid.* 21.

pretation he justifies by a curious explanation of Jarim, or 'Ιαρείμ as he found it in the LXX. version.[1]

The second form of symbolical interpretation is that which has received general currency, and until lately has been the usual method of interpreting prophecy. It is what is commonly known as "the double sense." According to it, the historical sense is the primary meaning of the prophet, but beyond this obvious meaning there is a further reference to some more distant future event connected with Christianity or the end of the world. Whether the prophet himself meant or realised this further event, or it was rather the meaning of the Spirit who spoke through the prophet, was a question either not considered at all, or answered differently by different writers. It would be premature to consider whether, under any form or limitations, a double sense of a prophecy is admissible. I am now using the phrase as it is commonly accepted by theologians, according to which the secondary sense has no connexion with the primary sense except by type or symbol, and even that has not always been considered necessary. Thus understood, this and also the other form of symbolical interpretation already described both weaken very seriously, if they do not practically destroy, the whole argument from prophecy. For, with a little ingenuity, a prophetic prediction may be found for any event whatever, and the argument

[1] "Et bene addit nomen Jarim, quod est sylvester." He understood it as the Hebrew יְעָרִים, "woods," the word which we get in Kirjath-jearim, "the city of woods." The Vulgate, on the contrary, has "ultori."

comes to depend not so much on the prophet's foresight as on the apologist's cleverness in evolving interpretations.

It might be objected that we get very strange interpretations of prophecy in the New Testament itself. I suppose no commentator of the present day would seriously deny that Hosea by the words, "I called my son out of Egypt" (Hos. xi. 1), meant a reference to the exodus of the Israelites. How then is St Matthew right in referring them to the return of Joseph and Mary with the infant Saviour (Matt. ii. 15)? or how, again, is he right when he quotes a passage of Jeremiah which speaks poetically of Rachel in her tomb weeping over the Israelites slaughtered by their Babylonian conquerors, and refers it to the massacre of the innocents at Bethlehem (Jer. xxxi. 15; Matt. ii. 18)? How, again, are we to justify those explanations of prophecy in the New Testament which are based upon Greek mistranslations of the Hebrew?[1] If we accept such interpretations, are we logically justified, it may be asked, in rejecting, as forced or unnatural, a whole host of Patristic interpretations, which are, most of them, hardly more extravagant? To this there can be, it seems to me, only one answer that a fair or wise apologist of the present day can give. All such explanations are part of that system of allegorical interpretation which is at least as old as Christianity itself. The Christians themselves derived it from the Jews, and both parties naturally used it in

[1] See, for example, Acts ii. 31; Heb. x. 5.

perfect good faith in arguing for their religious systems. St Matthew quotes those prophecies in the early chapters of his Gospel because, according to the methods of thought prevalent in his own day, they were a strong argument in favour of the Messianic claims of Jesus. To us they are not a strong argument—on the whole their use as such is rather a stumbling-block. For atheists and sceptics they are obviously no argument at all. It is a foolish thing to use antiquated weapons to defend Christian truth. By such means we should neither convince a single unbeliever nor confirm our own faith. And what is the use of apologetics except for the one purpose or the other?

The opposite tendency, not to see Christ at all in the Old Testament, may be called the extreme result of the historical and critical spirit of the age, and of the method of interpretation to which it has given rise. To many minds the result is so repugnant that they are disposed to move the previous question, and to refuse to examine its claims. But this is unfair, and it is certainly unwise. If the reasoning is unsound, its unsoundness ought to be shewn up, for it must be dangerous. The apologist is the very last person who can afford to say, "I will have none of that method of arguing, because I do not know what it may lead me to." On the contrary, if he is wise, he will first examine its principles, and then, if they are sound, consider whether they are rightly applied. It is obviously most important to keep these two questions completely separate. It is of course perfectly reasonable and right to say, " the conclusions to which this method has sometimes led commentators are so serious, so upsetting to my rooted convictions, that I am specially bound to satisfy myself of its reasonableness, and will not be led astray by plausible but shallow arguments." But this is a very different thing from refusing to examine the argument. The more important the conclusions, the more important is it that the argument should be weighed with perfect thoroughness and absolute fairness.

Let us then for a moment leave out of consideration the conclusions which seem to follow from this method, or for which it has been sometimes made responsible, and consider the method itself. The principle is briefly this, that the meaning of a prophet is what he himself meant to say. To understand this, we must ascertain, as far as possible, all the circumstances of the prophet—his political surroundings, the religious ideas and practices of his times, the relation of his people to foreign Powers, and so on. The history, in fact, instead of being of minor importance, becomes at the very least the foundation, the starting-point of his discourses. To many this will seem so obvious as hardly to have required stating; but, as I have already pointed out, it has not been in the past the method usually employed. In fact, it is only quite lately that the history of the Jews has been either fully appreciated or clearly understood. The discovery of ancient monuments has made historical investigation more and more possible, and has given a new life to prophetic study. This has been combined with a more accurate knowledge of Hebrew philology. And what have been the immediate results? That instead of finding in the prophets, for the most part, strings of conundrums, into which each commentator has read his own meaning, we find language which, as a rule, is intelligible and real—full of life and full of beauty.

Briefly speaking, then, this method is justified both by its transparent reasonableness and by its general results. That it is the right one, the only one that can satisfy an intelligent seeker after truth, can hardly be questioned. If so, our first question is answered—the principle itself is sound. But what are we to say of the second? How about the application of the principle? Are we justified in saying, with some commentators, that the prophets know nothing and say nothing of Christ? Certainly not as an *a priori* statement. To one who believes in a supernatural revelation—we might say to one who believes in a personal God at all—it is antecedently possible that God may have revealed beforehand a perfectly clear knowledge of Christ and Christianity, and the prophets may have found occasions when contemporary events justified the foretelling of this more distant future. But it is a thing which cannot be decided by any *a priori* reasoning. We must examine the facts. The question is not what the prophets *might* have been empowered to say and *might* have thought fit to say, but what they *have* said. And to know this we must study the prophets from their own standpoint, and find out what they said and what they meant. If their words bear a natural reference to the known events of their own time, it is not likely that they intended them to be prophetic of future events which were to take place at a far-distant date, and in a way very different from that which they actually describe. It has, indeed, been sometimes argued that we have no right to limit the meaning of a prophecy to what the prophet meant. That in flights of deep spiritual feeling they may very probably have, so to speak, gone beyond themselves and uttered truths of which they only partially realised the full force. An analogy has even been drawn from the poets of our own day. What is the meaning, it has been urged, of Browning Societies, even during the lifetime of the poet, if not to seek out these deeper significations of which the poet himself was only partly conscious? There is a certain degree of truth, no doubt, in this. But when examined what does it amount to? Simply this, that, in persons of deep feeling especially, ideas and mental images are not always capable of being consciously thought out or expressed in clearly defined language. This will be generally admitted. But it surely does not warrant us in searching for meanings altogether different from, or only remotely analogous to, what was evidently present to the mind of the prophet. It will not, for example, justify any of those extravagant New Testament interpretations of prophecy which we have already referred to.

But at this point it would be well to notice a distinction, which must be clearly made if we are to avoid confusion of thought. It is one thing to say that the prophets actually foresaw and foretold Christ, quite another thing to say that they foretold a state of things, which as a fact was fulfilled, though not precisely as they expected, in Christ and Christianity. And if I was right in what I said of the limits of their temporal predictions, [this is all that we have any reason to expect.

Let us now take the prophets into our hands, and let them speak for themselves. The first result of an independent study is of necessity negative. We cannot, try as we will, forget the interpretations to which we have been accustomed from our childhood. (1) The first thing that inevitably strikes us, is that many prophecies which we have been taught to regard as Messianic have a direct and obvious meaning *in the events of the prophet's time.* We have a typical example of this in the Immanuel prophecy of Isa. vii. 14. This passage was a bone of contention between the Jews and the Christians as early as the time of Justin Martyr, and the arguments on both sides are fully given in his Dialogue with Trypho.[1] The Christians, probably deriving their argument from St Matthew i. 23, maintained that the words translated in the Greek Bible, "The virgin shall conceive," &c.,

---

[1] See *Dial. c. Tryph.*, 43, 66, 67-84.

were a prophetic announcement of the birth of Christ
from His virgin mother. The Jews, on the other
hand, maintained that the word עלמה did not necessarily mean a virgin, but only a young woman, and
that the prophet intended to refer to Hezekiah. The
point was considered to be of such importance that,
under the auspices of Aquila or Onkelos, a new Greek
translation of the Bible was made, in which the word
νεᾶνις was substituted for the παρθένος of the pre-
Christian LXX. version.[1] Hebrew scholars are now
pretty generally agreed that, so far as the word עלמה
is concerned, Trypho was right, and that it is hardly
conceivable that Isaiah would have used an ambiguous
word, had he meant the virgin-birth to be the sign
intended. And if we study the whole passage without
prejudice, we find far more to be said on the same
side. It becomes obvious that the point of the sign
is not so much anything miraculous in the birth of
the child, as the fact that his early years would be
marked by two remarkable events—(*a*) A desolation
of the country, which is signified by the simplest food
being made necessary through the devastations of a
foreign enemy—the child is to eat butter and honey
instead of cultivated fruits and cereals ; (*b*) The crushing of the power of Rezin and Pekah by Assyria
—" For before the child shall know to refuse the evil
and choose the good, the land, whose two kings thou
abhorrest, shall be forsaken." Moreover, the sign is
given in wrath. The fulfilment of these prophecies

---

[1] See Eusebius, *Eccles. Hist.* v. 8 (quotation from Irenæus).

was to be to Ahaz the sign of God's judgment on himself: "Yahweh shall bring upon thee, and upon thy people, and upon thy father's house, days that have not come from the day that Ephraim departed from Judah; even the king of Assyria." And there follows a vivid but highly poetical description of the devastation of the southern kingdom. On the hills once famous for their priceless vines and their crops there was to be nothing but briars and thorns; and men would have to get what scanty subsistence they could by shooting wild animals, or grazing a few cattle and sheep on the scanty pasturage among the thickets. The general line of thought is this:—You and your advisers are secretly seeking an alliance with Assyria to ward off the attacks of Syria and Ephraim. You affect a pious reverence for God, but your whole attitude shews utter distrust and impiety. God will punish you as you deserve. Your plan, as you devise it, will be perfectly successful, but the very power which you have called in to crush your foes will crush yourself. This is the chief line of thought. I am far from saying that it exhausts the whole meaning. But see what life and spirit is given to the whole chapter when so understood! I know of no passage in the Old Testament which more completely vindicates the superiority of the new method of interpretation to the old. If it be asked, Does such an interpretation preclude a Messianic reference? it must be answered, Not necessarily; but this much may certainly be said: That if Isaiah was speaking in ver. 14 of the birth of the

Messiah, he must have believed that the Messiah was very shortly to appear. Such is the view to which several of the most able of modern critics actually incline. The opinion of Delitzsch on this point is particularly interesting. In his early Commentary on Isaiah he exhausted his ingenuity in endeavouring, very unsatisfactorily, to shew how the birth of Christ, or rather the prophet's prediction of the birth of Christ, could be a sign to Ahaz. But in later life this great pillar of conservative criticism, without losing any of his religious faith or religious earnestness, felt bound to accept the principles of the new critical school, and he accepted them with perfect frankness. The following remark on the passage in question occurs in his lectures on Messianic prophecy delivered in 1877, and published shortly before his death:—"Those who think that Immanuel, because he was a child of the Assyrian time of judgment, could not be the Messiah, fail to recognise the law of perspective shortening to which all prophecy, even that concerning Jesus Christ Himself in the Gospels is subject. Isaiah lived to see that the expectation of the parousia of the Messiah in the time of the Assyrian oppression was not fulfilled; nevertheless he was not ashamed of his prophecy, and did not withdraw it."[1]

Let us take another example in some ways still more striking. We have in Jer. iv. 23-26 a passage which seems to speak in unequivocal language of the end of the world. The earth or land returns to

[1] *Messianic Prophecies*, Eng. Trans., p. 141.

primitive chaos; light disappears; man is no more; and birds fly away. A desolate wilderness takes the place of fruitful vegetation. But after this the prophecy passes into what is evidently a description of a country ravaged by a foreign enemy. The destruction of cities, the flight of the inhabitants to places of refuge, the desolation of the country,—all are plainly depicted. And interwoven with this, again, is a description, half poetical, half perhaps literal, of the way in which heaven and earth take part in the judgment of God. "For this shall the earth mourn, and the heavens above be black; because I have spoken it, I have purposed it, and I have not repented, neither will I turn back from it" (28). Now what is the conclusion derived from a careful study of this whole passage? It is clearly this, that however much the language of Jeremiah lends itself to an eschatological sense, what he has directly in view is the invasion of a foreign enemy, which he foretells as a judgment from God. Now if these first few chapters belong, as is commonly supposed, to the early days of Jeremiah, it seems probable that this vision of Jeremiah, so terrible as seeming to predict nothing less than the end of the world, was due to an imminent invasion of the Scythians, which in fact proved so little disastrous to Palestine that, except in this passage and perhaps in the prophet Zephaniah, it left no permanent traces on Jewish literature.[1] We have again a parallel instance in the 24th chapter of Isaiah. There,

[1] See Cheyne, *Jeremiah: His Life and Times*, chap. 4.

in the midst of a passage which speaks in the strongest language of what appears to be the desolation of the whole world, there is quite unexpectedly a reference to the destruction of a particular city (ver. 10), and this is followed by a characteristic prediction of the salvation of a remnant. Now these are no isolated instances. We find the same fact over and over again. What seems at first sight to refer to a state of things utterly unlike the prophet's own surroundings is frequently found, on examination, to refer directly to events of his own time, and events of which, in the context, he is evidently speaking.

(2) Again, if we study the context of what are more obviously Messianic predictions in the wide sense of the expression, even these we find, in the prophet's view, to be closely dependent upon some impending historical event. Let us take, *e.g.*, the great prophecy of Isa. ix. 1-7. This is perhaps the most remarkable Messianic prophecy in the Old Testament. Now, if we read this in connexion with the two previous chapters, we then see the dark background against which the brilliant picture of the future is evidently drawn. But what is this darkness, in contrast to which the light of chap. ix. suddenly bursts in upon us? It is clearly the condition of the people in the time of the prophet, probably during the reign of Ahaz, when they were given over to the grossest superstition and idolatry, and the prophet in vain tried to arouse in the people, as a whole, some feeling of religious patriotism. Now let us suppose for a

moment that Isaiah distinctly foresaw Christ as he afterwards really was. His prediction would then amount to this:—This gross superstition, these constant political intrigues, must go on for some centuries. Then one will come who will reveal truths which, after a further lapse of many centuries, will be so infused into the hearts of all nations that they will recognise Him as their spiritual King, and in the end there will be universal peace under His government. But is this what his language naturally suggests? To think that such was the mind of Isaiah is to rob the prophecy of that present hope which evidently inspired him.

The detailed discussion of this prophecy we must reserve for a future paper; but is it not at least evident that Isaiah foresaw the golden age of his people in the near future?

We find the same thing in the prophet Jeremiah. The most marked Messianic prophecy of that prophet, at least in the narrower sense of the expression, is that which English Churchmen naturally associate with the Sunday before Advent, xxiii. 5, 6: " Behold, the days come, saith Yahweh, that I will raise unto David a righteous Shoot, and He shall reign as king, and deal wisely, and shall execute judgment and justice in the land. In His days Judah shall be saved, and Israel shall dwell safely; and this is His name whereby He shall be called, The Lord is our Righteousness." Now if we examine the context before and after these words, we shall see that

Jeremiah has in his mind the Restoration from the Captivity. The prophecy is directed against the shepherds that destroyed and scattered the sheep of God's pasture. By these are meant, according to a common Hebrew metaphor, the rulers and guides of the people, probably in the widest sense of the term,—principally the kings, but also their counsellors, the priests and prophets, and those generally who held an unofficial position in Church or State. These unfaithful shepherds are, in the restored state, to be supplanted by shepherds who shall really feed the flock. The centre of this new government is to be a king distinguished for prudence and righteousness, who stands in contrast to the foolish and selfish kings of Jeremiah's time. In the days to come people will look back with gratitude upon the Restoration as the greatest act of national deliverance. It will take the place formerly occupied in their minds by the deliverance from Egypt. "Therefore behold the days come, saith Yahweh, that they shall no more say, As Yahweh liveth, which brought up the children of Israel out of the land of Egypt; but as Yahweh liveth, which brought up and which led the seed of the house of Israel out of the north country, and from all the countries whither I had driven them; and they shall dwell in their own land." Now supposing that Jeremiah had in his mind a definite conception of the personality of Christ and His work at some distant time, is it likely that he would have so focussed his thoughts upon the mere fact of national deliverance? Would he not almost certainly have made some part of that work itself the ground for national gratitude ? As it is, the prophecy of the righteous king is inseparably bound up with the return of the exiles.

And now let me recapitulate the results to which this inquiry has led us :—(1) We have found it necessary to reject, honestly and unreservedly, a method of interpreting prophecy which, though it has held the field for many centuries, is now more and more coming to be felt irrational, and for those who feel so dishonest, in any case useless for apologetic purposes. (2) We have made it more possible to come to terms with those whose principles of interpretation are rational, and therefore so far right, but seem to ignore, or at least fail to appreciate fully, the more spiritual and religious side of the character and utterances of the prophets. For the very first necessity in controversy is to understand what our antagonists mean, and to agree frankly on all points in which we feel that they are right. If we have travelled so far on the road with them, we shall better see where, how and why our paths diverge. The rejection of the Messianic interpretation may be a very serious difference, or it may prove to be little more than a question of words,—in any case, a difference often of degree rather than of kind. If we wish to shew that we are right in accepting any Messianic interpretations, we must do so on those same grounds of sober reason which have led us to reject many which we now know to be false.

But if we would be candid inquirers, we must be prepared to be convinced as well as to convince. The opinions of earnest religious thinkers have changed marvellously in the last forty years. Is it reasonable to expect that they will not continue to change in the next forty? Some of my readers will be old enough to remember the storm of indignation that was excited by a book by Rowland Williams, called *Rational Godliness*. In answering some of the charges made against him by his critics he used these words: "What Bishop Butler conceded hypothetically, that all prophecies of Christ in the Old Testament referred primarily to the Jewish people, kings, or prophets, must, in the present state of biblical criticism, be frankly accepted as a fact."[1] Rowland Williams was many years before his time; but since that day a patient study of the Bible has been gradually influencing the mind of Englishmen, and it will probably not be long before this principle is accepted as an axiom of prophetic study.

"But will the study of the Bible mean for ever the rooting-out and destruction of old ideas?" This is the cry of the timid theologian. Surely not. The elimination of what is untrue, the rectification of what is distorted—this is, in order of time, no doubt, the first work of criticism, but it is not its chief work. If it has first to pull down what is built on insecure foundations, it is that it may build up on surer foun-

---

[1] Extract from a letter quoted in *Biographical Sketches* (Kegan Paul), p. 102.

dations what is lasting and true. And what is true in a larger sense of criticism generally in its relation to Jewish history, is true in a special sense of the argument from prophecy. We must get rid of what is unsound in that argument if it is to have any real convincing power. We must get rid of false or forced interpretations of prophecy before we can get at the true meaning. And from that meaning alone we must draw our arguments. We have seen that the temporal event not merely suggested some future prediction, but is the root and foundation of all prophecy. To what extent, and under what limitations, we have a right to say that the prophets looked beyond this event and foresaw the more distant future, is a question which demands a dispassionate inquiry. And this is what we shall have to consider in the following chapters.

CHAPTER V

THE MATERIAL ELEMENTS OF THE MESSIANIC HOPE

" There shall be abundance of corn in the earth upon the top of the mountains; the fruit thereof shall shake like Lebanon: and they of the city shall flourish like grass of the earth."—Ps. lxxii. 16.

IT is now time to take a general view of the great Messianic hope, which found its expression in the books of the Old Testament, and more especially in the Prophets. The most natural course, perhaps, would be first to arrange in order those prophecies which seem to speak of facts connected with the Christ of our four Gospels, and then to trace, if possible, the gradual growth of the Messianic conception. But such a method is beset with many practical difficulties. (1) The present state of Biblical criticism does not permit us to draw such a chronological outline with sufficient exactness, and were we on the other hand to take it from the present arrangement of Old Testament books and sections, it would be extremely misleading. (2) Such a method would not satisfy the needs of at least many a thoughtful inquirer. What he most wants to know is not—For how many facts related in the Gospels can I find, or seem to find, scattered predictions or allusions in the Old Testament? but this—What portraits do the prophets draw of the great Coming

Age, and to what extent and in what ways were their expectations justified by Christ and Christianity? (3) To tear the so-considered Christian elements of prophecy out of their contexts and string them together for such a purpose, is to rob them in a great measure of their vitality and their beauty, and often to obscure their meaning. It was out of the present and temporal that the more distant and more spiritual grew, and we must realise and understand the former before we can fully appreciate the latter.

For these reasons I shall adopt what seems a more feasible and satisfactory plan. I shall attempt to collect some of those broader and more frequent features of prophecy which mainly contributed to form what has been, and is, the great hope of the Jewish nation. The prophets often compared themselves to watchmen. From their tower they looked out on the great world about them and beyond them. Immediately in front lay the lowlands, often dark, gloomy, monotonous. Beyond rose the beautiful but hazy outline of the distant hills, tipped here and there, it might be, with the rosy tints of the coming dawn. But if we are to understand the prophet's landscape, we must not look too exclusively at the rays of distant heavenly light, but take also into our view the dark and gloomy foreground, which at times intercepted the brilliant future from their view. It is this double aspect of the prophet's mental view, this mixture of light and shade, which has given such very different impressions of their character and their work. They have been described by some as gloomy pessimists, by others as utopian optimists. Each statement expresses a truth. The age of the prophets was for the most part an age of moral and religious corruption, and also very usually one of impending disaster. To cry out against present wrongs, and foretell God's immediate judgments, was the first and most pressing part of their work, hence their pessimism; but there were very few who did not look beyond this darker prospect to some brighter future for their nation, which the purifying power of judgment should make possible. Herein lay their optimism.

But it is not with the present surroundings of the prophets, nor with the impending disasters of the immediate future, that we have now to do. These changed with the special characters of the time. We have rather to consider those elements of hope which we find repeated under various aspects in different prophets, and which tended to pass into what we may call a sort of prophetic tradition. Among these, if what I have been saying is true, we shall hardly be surprised to find that material blessings occupy an important place. And it is to these that I purpose to confine myself in the present paper.

i. First among them we may place the fertility of the soil and agricultural prosperity. These naturally entered very largely into the national hope. The Jews were originally, it seems, a nation of small peasant proprietors. The land, at the present day dry and sterile from want of water, was in Biblical times proverbial for its fertility, "a land flowing with milk and honey." Near the coast were the extensive cornfields of the lowlands (*Shephélah*); west of these the mountains of Ephraim were celebrated for their vines; to the south were the rich pasture-lands of Judah. But the agricultural industry was waning in the age of the great prophets. Constant wars had too often devastated the country, and wellnigh paralysed agricultural enterprise. The crops, too, very frequently suffered from natural disasters, locusts, mildew, and drought. Moreover, the old hereditary system of land tenure was breaking down, even in the more conservative northern kingdom. The land was passing out of the old families into the hands of large mercenary-minded proprietors—men who, in the scathing language of the prophets, ground the face of the poor, and sold the needy for a pair of shoes (Isa. iii. 15 ; Amos. ii. 6).

In contrast to such a state of things, a time of unexampled, if not even miraculous, agricultural prosperity was foretold by almost every prophet in succession. In the Book of Amos, the herdman of Tekoa, it is not surprising to find such a promise forming the most conspicuous feature of that one vision of national hope with which the book closes. "Behold, the days come, saith Yahweh, that the plowman shall overtake the reaper, and the treader of grapes him that soweth seed ; and the mountains shall drop sweet wine, and all the hills shall melt" (Amos ix. 13). But we should not have expected such promises of rural blessedness in the townsman and polished courtier, Isaiah. And yet we do find them frequently enough. Thus, in contrast to the famine which should be sent as a punishment for the luxury of the men and the immodest vanity of the women, he foretells a day when " the shoot of Yahweh shall be beautiful and glorious, and the fruit of the land excellent and comely for them that are escaped of Israel " (Isa. iv. 2).[1] Later on, in xxx. 23, 24, in the midst of that strange succession of Messianic hopes, which bursts upon our view so suddenly after the denunciations in the earlier part of the chapter, he draws a picture of rural life, in which corn would be so abundant that even the oxen and young asses that ploughed the land would be fed on the very choicest meal.

The melancholy Jeremiah and the stern Ezekiel both find room for the same theme. Jeremiah, in the only complete picture which he draws of post-captivity life (chap. xxxi.) foretells that the virgin daughter of Israel shall again plant "vineyards upon the mountains of Samaria " (5), and describes how the people in Zion " shall flow together unto the goodness of Yahweh, to the corn, and to the wine, and to the oil, and to the young of the flock and of the herd " (12). In a somewhat similar strain, Ezekiel (xxxvi. 30) promises to the land the fertility of Paradise : " I will multiply

---

[1] The word צמח has been here explained, as in Zech. iii. 8, of the Messianic King who was to shoot up from the royal house of David (cf. Isa. xi. 1). But the context makes it best to refer it to the crops of the soil regarded as Yahweh's possession.

the fruit of the tree, and the increase of the field, that ye shall receive no more the reproach of famine among the nations;" so that they that passed by would say, "This land that was desolate is become like the Garden of Eden" (35).

The same thought is repeated by the deutero-Isaiah in chap. li. 3: "For Yahweh hath comforted Zion; He hath comforted all her waste places, and hath made her wilderness like Eden, and her desert like the garden of Yahweh." But figures of this kind are so often employed by him metaphorically, that to press the literal meaning of the words would be, perhaps, to ignore the poetry of the passage. Yet it seems probable that a promise of natural productiveness is at least included. In chap. lxv. 21, 22, one of the privileges of the "new heavens and the new earth" is that the people would be able to plant vineyards, and eat the fruit themselves, instead of its falling a prey to their enemies (cf. lxii. 8, 9). Finally, in the last age of Hebrew prophecy, the priestly prophet Malachi promises the richest agricultural blessings on the condition that men will give God the tithes which He claims: "Bring ye the whole tithe into the storehouse, that there may be meat in Mine house, and prove Me now herewith, saith Yahweh of hosts, if I will not open you the windows of heaven, and pour you out a blessing, that there shall not be room enough to receive it. And I will rebuke the devourer for your sakes, and he shall not destroy the fruits of your ground; neither shall your vine cast her fruit before the time in the field, saith Yahweh of hosts. And all nations shall call you happy ; for ye shall be a delightsome land, saith Yahweh of hosts" (Mal. iii. 10-12). Many other examples of the kind might be added, if necessary. The point here contended for is not merely that the several prophets foretold at different periods future seasons of plenty, but that in almost every instance the promise is so blended with other Messianic thoughts, that it clearly formed an essential part of the prophet's great future hope.

ii. A second common feature among the material blessings of the promised future is the enormous increase of the population. This was a hope which had its roots in the early history of the people. When Hosea foretold (i. 10) that "the number of the children of Israel" should be "as the sand of the sea, which cannot be measured or numbered," he was but echoing the promise to Abraham in Gen. xxii. 17.[1] Other prophets express the same thought by various figures. Thus, *e.g.*, the deutero-Isaiah in chap. liv. 1-8 compares Jerusalem desolated during the Captivity to a barren woman, who is sudddenly blessed with children! "Sing, O barren, thou that didst not bear ; break forth into singing and cry aloud thou that didst not travail with child : for more are the children of the desolate than the children of the married wife, saith Yahweh." In Isa. xlix. 20, 21, there is a some-

---

[1] According to Kuenen (*Hexateuch*, Engl. Transl. p. 244) a passage belonging to the eighth century, and therefore about contemporary with Hosea, but even so, it is probably founded on an earlier tradition.

what similar thought of a bereaved mother finding herself surrounded by children so numerous that their home is not sufficient for them.

These prophecies prepare us for the still bolder figure which describes the sudden springing up of the people in the redeemed Israel as a resurrection from the dead. The best known example is the striking vision of the dry bones in Ezek. xxxvii. The prophet, it is true, himself apparently explains this of the revival of the people, who were dead and buried as it were in Babylon, into a new and vigorous life. "Then He said unto me, Son of man, these bones are the whole house of Israel: behold, they say, Our bones are dried up, and our hope is lost: we are clean cut off. Therefore prophesy, and say unto them, Thus saith the Lord Yahweh: Behold, I will open your graves, and cause you to come up out of your graves, O my people, and I will bring you into the land of Israel."[1] But this last verse seems to imply some further meaning, which is certainly suggested by the general character of the description. Great stress is laid, for example, on the fact that the bones are "very many," and that when they are restored to life they become "an exceeding great army." It was as though the Captivity was to be entirely wiped out, and all those who had died in Babylon were to share with the survivors the new national life.

The same idea is expressed rather differently by the probably somewhat earlier prophet to whom we owe

[1] Ezek. xxxvii. 11, 12.

that unique prophecy, Isa. xxiv.-xxvii. In xxvi. 13-19, there is a strong contrast between the utter and hopeless destruction of Israel's enemies and the sudden increase of their own people. Then follows a description of the half-desperate yearnings of the people which should precede the fulfilment of this promise. They are compared to the agonising, but for a long while fruitless, birth-throes of a travailing woman. But suddenly the pains are over, and with one of those rapid transitions of thought so characteristic of these chapters, the prophet describes the upspringing of the dead of Israel. "Thy dead shall live, my dead bodies shall arise, Awake and sing, ye that dwell in the dust: for thy dew is as the dew of herbs, and the earth shall cast forth the dead" (Isa. xxvi. 19).[1] Many commentators take both these passages as conscious predictions of the resurrection of the body; and as far as the last passage is concerned, there is much to be said for this view. The promise in xxv. 8, "He hath swallowed up death for ever," is evidently part of the same prophecy. But even these words cannot be intended to express, what taken literally they imply, a universal resurrection; for they are followed in the very next paragraph by a woful description of the destruction of the typical enemy Moab at God's hand. If a resurrection is intended in the 26th chapter, it is at least with two important limitations. (1) It is

---

[1] Dr Driver (*Isaiah and his Times*, p. 123) takes the first two clauses as a prayer, "Let thy dead live! let my dead bodies arise!" but this does not affect the general meaning of the passage.

expressly confined to Israel. The foreign lords which had had dominion over them "are dead, . . . they shall not rise." (2) It is connected in the prophet's thought with some definite historical event, in all probability the Restoration which should follow the taking of Babylon (Isa. xxv. 2).

iii. The last material feature in the Messianic hope which we shall notice concerns the future relations of the redeemed nation to other peoples—(1) to the northern kingdom of Samaria; (2) to foreign nations generally. On the first point we must not be misled by the term Israel. The word is not used by the prophets exclusively, or even generally, of the northern kingdom only, but often either of the whole nation, or, after the captivity of the north, of the southern kingdom alone, as the remaining representative of the whole nation. Thus the "house of Israel" is Ezekiel's favourite expression for the Jews, and in Mal. ii. 11 we actually find Judah and Israel used as synonymous terms. "Judah hath dealt treacherously, and an abomination is committed in Israel and in Jerusalem." Had this been always realised, we might have been spared a good deal of the modern literature about the lost tribes.

But in many passages there can be no doubt of the application of the word Israel to the northern kingdom. The prophets never countenanced the jealousy which so frequently existed between the north and the south, and was one of the chief causes of national weakness. The southern prophets, though they dwell mostly on the glories of the future Jerusalem, its monarchy and its worship, yet for the most part shew that they included the northern kingdom in the promises of future blessedness. Thus Amos, the missionary prophet to the north, pointed to the day when the breaches in the tabernacle of David were to be closed up (ix. 11). Isaiah, in the great prophecy of the Branch, foretells that the outcasts of Israel are to be assembled as well as the dispersed of Judah from the four corners of the earth, and then goes on to say, "The envy also of Ephraim shall depart, and they that vex Judah shall be cut off: Ephraim shall not envy Judah, and Judah shall not vex Ephraim," (Isa. xi., 12, 13). Again, Jeremiah, in a passage already quoted, speaks of the virgin daughter of Israel as once more about to plant vineyards on the mountains of Samaria, where the whole context shews that the northern tribes are intended.

The writer of the middle portion of the Book of Zechariah, who wrote before the captivity of Judah, which he does not appear to have contemplated, speaks still more explicitly of the Restoration of Israel, and evidently implies that Judah would be thus strengthened by the help of her natural allies: "And I will strengthen the house of Judah, and I will save the house of Joseph, and I will bring them again; for I have mercy upon them: and they shall be as though I had not cast them off; for I am Yahweh their God, and I will hear them." And this was to be brought about by the humiliation of the two great enemies of the people, the Assyrians on the east, and the Egyptians on the south. "And he shall pass through the sea of affliction, and shall smite the waves in the sea, and all the depths of the Nile shall dry up; and the pride of Assyria shall be brought down, and the sceptre of Egypt shall depart away." (Zech. x. 6-12)[1]. Similarly the future union of the two kingdoms under one shepherd, God's servant David, is prefigured by Ezekiel under the symbol of the two sticks bound together (xxxvii. 15-28).

The general impression left us by the prophets who wrote before the return of the Jewish captives is that they believed that there would be a simultaneous restoration of all the tribes of Israel and Judah from wherever they might happen to be in exile. This, at any rate, was the expectation of Isaiah, as we see from the prophecy already referred to on this subject (xi. 11): "And it shall come to pass in that day, that Yahweh shall set His hand again the second time to recover the remnant of His people, which shall remain from Assyria, and from Egypt, and from Pathros, and from Cush, and from Elam, and from Shinar, and from Hamath, and from the islands of the sea." Similarly, the prophet of the Captivity speaks of ships of Tarshish as bringing the sons of the Jewish people from far, which cannot of course refer to the Babylonian captives (Isa. lx. 9).

[1] In ver. 6 the R.V. reads וְהוֹשִׁיבֹתִים "I will make them return," for the Massoretic וְהוֹשַׁבְתִּים "I will settle them," cf. LXX. κατοικιῶ αὐτούς. But in any case the return of the exiles is obviously implied.

There is, however, a somewhat obscure passage in Ezek. iv., where a different belief seems to be expressed. According to the reading of the Hebrew text of vv. 5, 6, and 9, the captivity of Israel is to last 390 years, from its commencement presumably, whereas the captivity of Judah, calculated it would appear from the final siege of Jerusalem by Nebuchadrezzar, is to last forty. This makes the restoration of Israel at least 200 years later than that of Judah. If, however, we adopt the reading of the LXX., the restoration of Judah and Israel becomes simultaneous. In v. 4, LXX. adds πεντήκοντα καὶ ἑκατὸν; in vv. 5 and 9 they read ἐνενήκοντα καὶ ἑκατὸν in place of Hebrew, שלש מאות ותשעים; that is to say, 150 in v. 4, 190 in vv. 5 and 9 instead of 390. According to this reading, the 150 years would refer to the time which intervened between the commencement of the Exile of Israel and the time when that of Judah commenced, the remaining 40 years to the time that both Israel and Judah would still remain in captivity, 190 to the whole predicted duration of the captivity of Israel. The 150 years is probably to be reckoned from the first captivity of those in the northern and north-easterly districts of Israel by Tiglath-pileser after the death of Pekah, in 734, to the final destruction of Jerusalem by Nebuchadrezzar in 588. The exact number would thus be, according to Jewish reckoning, 147, so that 150 regarded as a round number is practically accurate. On the other hand, starting from the point reached at the close of the

150 years, namely the destruction of Jerusalem, and calculating to the actual Restoration, we find that the Captivity lasted, according to Jewish reckoning, 51 years instead of 40, the time assigned to it here and by implication also in xxix. 12. This difference between the anticipated and actual duration of the Captivity, while it cannot cause any serious difficulty to one who studies the prophets without preconceived opinions as to the extent of their foreknowledge, is of considerable critical value. It shews that the LXX. translators do not appear to have altered the numbers to make them square with history, and their readings here, therefore, should have great weight as according with the general tenor of Hebrew prophecy on this subject.

The simultaneous restoration of Israel and Judah is predicted most unequivocally by Ezekiel's contemporary, Jeremiah: "In those days the house of Judah shall walk with the house of Israel, and they shall come together out of the land of the north to the land that I gave for an inheritance unto your fathers" (iii. 18). It has sometimes been objected that the prophecies of the restoration of Israel, in the narrower sense of the word, have never been fulfilled, and that therefore either the prophecies await some still future fulfilment, or, as is more often supposed, that they must be understood in a spiritual and not the literal sense: but what right have we, for the sake of any such *a priori* view about the nature of prophetic foreknowledge, to wrest the obvious meaning of the prophet's language?

The attitude in which the Jews were to be placed to foreign nations in the Great Future is more difficult to summarise, because it is treated in a somewhat different spirit by different prophets.

1. Sometimes the thought is merely that the Jews, and Jerusalem especially, will, under the protection of Yahweh, be safe from the attacks of foreign powers. This thought is expressed by Isaiah (xxxiii. 20, 21) in two figures, of which the last was suggested, it has been thought, by the situation of the Egyptian No, surrounded by canals.[1] "Look upon Zion, the city of our solemnities: thine eyes shall see Jerusalem a quiet habitation, a tent that shall not be removed, the stakes whereof shall never be plucked up, neither shall any of the cords thereof be broken. But there Yahweh shall be with us in majesty, a place of broad rivers and streams; wherein shall go no galley with oars, neither shall gallant ship pass thereby." So, too, when in Ezekiel (xxxviii., xxxix.) the countless hordes of Gog come up against the mountains of Israel, they are to be slain by Yahweh with "an overflowing shower, and great hailstones, fire, and brimstone" (Ezek. xxxviii. 22).

2. Sometimes, with some brighter promise for foreign nations generally the thought of the destruction of a special enemy is painfully mingled. Thus the writer of Isa. xxiv.-xxvii., after speaking in xxv. 7 of the

---

[1] The reason for this view is the use of the word יְאֹרִים (the plural of the word regularly used of the river Nile), which might be used of canals connected with the Nile. See Delitzsch, *in loco*.

destruction "in this mountain of the face of the covering that is cast over all peoples, and the veil that is spread over all nations," turns to speak of the utter annihilation of Moab, trodden down like straw in the water of the dunghill. There are few passages in the Old Testament of greater dramatic grandeur than the vision with which Isa. lxiii. opens, " Who is this that cometh from Edom, with dyed garments from Bozrah ? this that is glorious in his apparel, marching in the greatness of his strength ? " " I that speak in righteousness, mighty to save." " Wherefore art thou red in thine apparel, and thy garments like him that treadeth in the winefat ? " " I have trodden the winepress alone ; and of the people there was no man with me: yea, I trod them in mine anger, and trampled them in my fury ; and their lifeblood is sprinkled upon my garments, and I have stained all my raiment. For the day of vengeance was in mine heart, and the year of my redeemed is come." And yet these thoughts of vengeance are in dark contrast to the bright promises made to the nations in ch. lx. There was one foe whose conduct Jacob never could forgive, that elder brother who, in the day of Jerusalem, had said, " Down with it, down with it, even to the ground." And both prophet and psalmist were only too ready to join in the un-Christian wish : " Happy shall he be that taketh thy children and dasheth them against the stones."

3. Often the thought is the brighter one, that the nations will be led by some single act of God's primi-

tive justice to recognise His sovereignty. To take one striking example out of many. In Isa. xviii. the result of the slaughter of the Assyrian army was to be that the Ethiopians would offer themselves as a present to Yahweh of hosts.

4. Again, the Messianic era is described as one of international peace. "In the latter days," according to a very early prophecy quoted by Isaiah and Micah, "Yahweh shall judge between the nations, and shall reprove many peoples: and they shall beat their swords into plowshares, and their spears into pruning-hooks: nation shall not lift up sword against nation, neither shall they learn war any more."[1] In Isa. ix. 1-7, this peace is the direct consequence of their deliverance from their oppressor, probably Assyria,[2] after which the very recollection of war would be distasteful, and the soldiers would burn their clothes. "For every boot of the booted warrior, and the garments rolled in blood, shall even be for burning, for fuel of fire." This is also the case in Zech. ix. 9-17, where the promise of peace is strangely blended with the notes of war.

5. Most frequently the attitude of the nations is that of ready and willing submission. They are described as bringing back the captive Israelites to their homes, as in Isa. xiv. 2, and in xlix. 22 the prophet of the Captivity expands the promise of

---

[1] Isa. ii. 2-4; Micah iv. 1-3. The context makes it impossible to suppose that it is original in Isaiah. It might be so in Micah, except that Jeremiah (xxvi. 18) refers to the context in Micah as uttered in the days of Hezekiah, whereas the prophecy seems in Isaiah to belong to the reign of Jotham or Ahaz at latest.

[2] Cf. x. 24-27.

Isa. xi. 12, "Thus saith the Lord Yahweh, Behold, I will lift up Mine hand to the nations, and set up Mine ensign to the peoples: and they shall bring thy sons in their bosom, and thy daughters shall be carried upon their shoulders." In the next verse they are described as doing homage to the Israelites: "They shall bow down to thee with their faces to the earth, and lick the dust of thy feet." Often the nations are represented as bringing gifts as a token of submission. Thus in Ps. lxxii. 10, the kings of Tarshish and of the isles are to bring presents; the kings of Sheba and Seba to offer gifts to the king. The nations even become the slaves of the Israelites, as in Isa. xiv. 2, "And the peoples shall take them, and bring them to their place: and the house of Israel shall possess them in the land of Yahweh for servants and for handmaids: and they shall take them captive, whose captives they were; and they shall rule over their oppressors." Many of these thoughts are combined in Isa. lx. The light which is to arise upon Israel is a signal for all nations to come and bring their offerings, and those who will not come are to be destroyed. It is true, of course, that here, as in many other similar passages, the act of homage is not to Israel merely, but to Yahweh; yet still it is to him as the God or King of Israel that the homage is rendered. This is very clearly brought out, for example, in the concluding verses of Zechariah (xiv. 16-21).

And so we reach the double thought (1) of a world-wide religion of which the temple is in Jerusalem, and

(2) of a world-wide empire of which Jerusalem is the capital (see esp. Ps. lxxxvii.). It is but seldom, if at all, that the prophets rise to the higher thought that all nations have equal religious and political rights in the sight of God. But at least the way is prepared for this conception by Amos ix. 7: "Have not I brought up Israel out of the land of Egypt, and the Philistines from Caphtor, and the Syrians from Kir?" We find also the converse of the same thought in the bitter sarcasm of Jeremiah: "Behold, the days come, saith Yahweh, that I will punish all them that are circumcised in their uncircumcision; Egypt, and Judah, and Edom, and the children of Ammon and Moab . . . for all the nations are uncircumcised, and all the house of Israel are uncircumcised in heart" (ix. 25, 26). And Isaiah foretells the time when at any rate the two great enemies of Israel shall have equal religious privileges: "In that day there shall be a highway out of Egypt to Assyria, and the Assyrian shall come into Egypt, and the Egyptian into Assyria, and the Egyptians shall worship with the Assyrians. In that day shall Israel be the third with Egypt and with Assyria, a blessing in the midst of the earth; for that Yahweh of hosts hath blessed them, saying, Blessed be Egypt My people, and Assyria the work of My hands, and Israel Mine inheritance" (xix. 23-25).

CHAPTER VI

THE RELIGIOUS ASPECT OF THE MESSIANIC HOPE

"Yahweh, who shall sojourn in Thy tabernacle? who shall dwell in Thy holy hill? He that walketh uprightly, and worketh righteousness, and speaketh truth in his heart."—Ps. xv. 1, 2.

I SPOKE in the last chapter of the material blessings that were comprised in the great hope of the Jews. In the present I wish to speak of its more definitely religious and spiritual aspects. This broad distinction is not very satisfactory, because, according to the prophets' way of looking at it, the hope was on all its sides religious. I mean that they realised intensely what we too often, from a want of their strong faith, hardly realise at all, that the material world was in its truest and fullest sense God's world, and were equally convinced that the Jews were in a very special way God's people. If, then, the nation was to be glorious and prosperous in the future, this was quite the natural result of God's love to His people, and of their faith and trust in Him. And yet the material and religious aspects of the promise are separable in thought, and, so long as we do not lose sight of the religious idea which lay at the root of the whole, it is convenient for the purpose of discussion to separate them. It is convenient also to make a further distinction between what can never be separated in fact without serious loss—the external and formal side of religion on the one hand, and the inward and spiritual on the other.

I. To begin with the former. The prophets' ideal of religious worship was, roughly speaking, a development of existing forms, rather than a new departure. (1). One of its most prominent features is the absolute destruction of idols. This is represented either as the voluntary act of the people, or the direct or indirect work of their enemies, or again, as a thing done by God Himself. Thus Isaiah speaks of the people as so overpowered by "the terror of Yahweh," and "the glory of His majesty, when He ariseth to shake mightily the earth," that they cast away their "idols of silver, and idols of gold... to the moles and to the bats" (ii. 19, 20; comp. xxx. 22). Another prophet makes the destruction of idols the condition on which alone Jacob could expect to receive forgiveness of sins: "Therefore by this shall the iniquity of Jacob be purged; and this is all the fruit of taking away his sin; when he maketh all the stones of the altar as chalkstones that are beaten in sunder, so that the Asherim and the sun-images shall rise no more" (Isa. xxvii. 9). Hosea gives a sarcastic description of the grief of the Israelites, people and priests alike, when their golden calf should be sent off as a tribute to the Assyrian king: "The inhabitants of Samaria shall be in terror for the calves of Beth-aven: for the people thereof shall mourn over it, and the priests thereof that rejoiced over it, for the glory thereof, because it is departed from it. It also shall be carried unto Assyria for a present to King Jareb: Ephraim shall receive shame, and Israel shall be ashamed of his own counsel" (x. 5, 6). Zephaniah speaks in a similar vein of Yahweh as famishing all the gods of the earth (ii. 11). That is to say, they are to die of starvation, because they have no longer any worshipper to give them food.

This predicted destruction of idols seems generally intended to include that of symbolical representations used in the worship of Yahweh where such still existed. Hosea's prophecy of the fate of the calves has already been quoted. Micah again expressly foretells the destruction of pillars or obelisks (v. 13). These, though, like the calves, in all probability a heathen form of symbolism, had, it seems, been introduced into the worship of Yahweh. This is shewn, as has been frequently pointed out, from Isa. xix. 19, which forms a remarkable exception to the usual denunciation of such objects. For he there speaks of a pillar to Yahweh, not only as a thing conceivable, but as a natural and proper symbol of worship. Hosea, too, seems to speak of a pillar as part of the ordinary paraphernalia of worship, of which the people would be deprived for a time as a punishment (iii. 4). These facts tend to shew that in the prophetic ideals of religious worship there is a gradual growth, and that the several prophets did not advance very far beyond the religious ideas of the time in which they lived.

(2) This becomes still more evident when we consider a second great feature of the future worship—its centralisation. The idea which presented itself most frequently to the prophet's mind was that Jerusalem would be the centre for the religious worship of the world, and this, generally at least, combined with the thought of the distinct inferiority of the nations. But the earlier prophets have nothing to say of such a centralisation. There is not a hint of it in Hosea and Amos. For in the last great prophecy of Amos (ix. 11-15), the tabernacle of David, whose breaches are to be restored, is not the Temple of Jerusalem, which had certainly no direct connexion with David, but the Davidic monarchy, which had been rent asunder by the political schism of Jeroboam. Nor does it form part of the religion of the future as Isaiah conceived it. The ancient prophecy which he quotes in chap. ii. 2-4 speaks, it is true, of the mountain of Yahweh's house as established in the top of the mountains, and all nations as flowing unto it. But the object of the gathering of the nations is not the ceremonial worship of Yahweh, but the learning of His law: "And many peoples shall go and say, Come ye, and let us go up to the mountain of Yahweh, to the house of the God of Jacob; and He will teach us of His ways, and we will walk in His paths: for out of Zion shall go forth the law, and the word of Yahweh from Jerusalem."

Isaiah himself has, perhaps, a somewhat similar thought in chap. xi., where he concludes the well-known symbolical picture of harmony and peace with the words, "They shall not hurt nor destroy in all My holy mountain: for the earth shall be full of the knowledge of Yahweh, as the waters cover the sea" (xi. 9). This might mean that the spiritual harmony which proceeds out of Mount Zion should spread itself over the earth. But it is at least quite as likely that the word הארץ here does not mean the world, but, according to its most frequent usage, the land of Palestine, and that "My holy mountain" does not mean Mount Zion, but the high land generally. So that both expressions are practically synonymous for Palestine. Thus we should get the natural thought that peace and harmony would reign everywhere in the country, because the knowledge of Yahweh would be universal. In any case there is nothing to point to Jerusalem as a centre of worship. On the contrary, in a passage already referred to (xix. 19-22) Isaiah foretells a time when sanctuaries to Yahweh should be established in Egypt.

It is when we come to the prophets of the Exile, and more especially to those of the Restoration, that we find the oft-repeated thought of the nations coming up to Jerusalem to do homage to the God of Israel, and to offer their gifts in His sanctuary. Some prophecies of this import I had occasion to mention in the last chapter. It will be sufficient now to add one significant passage from the prophet Haggai: "For thus saith Yahweh of hosts; Yet once, it is a little while, and I will shake the heavens, and the earth, and the sea, and the dry land; and I will shake all nations, and the desirable things of all nations shall come: and I will fill this house with glory, saith Yahweh of hosts. The silver is Mine, and the gold is Mine, saith Yahweh of hosts. The latter glory of this house shall be greater than the former, saith Yahweh of hosts: and in this place will I give peace, saith Yahweh of hosts" (ii. 6-9).

But out of this thought of a central sanctuary at Jerusalem, or perhaps we should say parallel with it, we can trace the development of a new thought which after all is very similar to that which we have already noticed in Isa. ii., viz., that this religious centre should send out its influence in all directions, till at last the whole world should become one great sanctuary of God. Some such idea is symbolized by Ezekiel in the vision of the waters which issued from under the threshold of the house, and fertilised the arid regions of the East (xlvii. 1-12). Zephaniah speaks of men as worshipping God every one from his place, even all the isles of the nations (ii. 11). Finally, in Malachi, we find the fullest development of the thought: "From the rising of the sun even unto the going down of the same My name is great among the Gentiles; and in every place incense is offered unto My name, and a pure offering: for My name is great among the Gentiles, saith Yahweh of hosts" (i. 11). Indeed, there is a hint in this passage of a decentralisation of a still more serious kind. The priests at Jerusalem were dishonouring God by a contempt for the holy ritual.

The Gentiles would not dare to act in this way, for among them Yahweh's name was still terrible. If the priests could not offer a more reverent service, better shut the temple doors, and offer no more sacrifice: "Oh that there were one among you that would shut the doors, that ye might not kindle fire on Mine altar in vain! I have no pleasure in you, saith Yahweh of hosts, neither will I accept an offering at your hand" (i. 10).

(3) As to the form of worship, it was to be a repetition, or in all probability an expansion, of what had already been in use. It was to have its priests (Jer. xxxi. 14) and its Levites (Jer. xxxiii. 21), its festivals (Zech. xiv. 19), its tithes (Mal. iii. 10), and sacrifices (Isa. lvi. 7). The first passage in Jeremiah here referred to is specially remarkable. He has just been describing in the loftiest strain the happy future in store for the people, in which they would not sorrow any more at all; and yet he is careful to tell us that God would "satiate the soul of the priests with fatness." Ezekiel is even more explicit: "For in Mine holy mountain, in the mountain of the height of Israel, saith the Lord Yahweh, there shall all the house of Israel, all of them, serve Me in the land: there will I accept them, and there will I require your offerings, and the firstfruits of your oblations, with all your holy things" (xx. 40). We may go even further than this, and say that in all probability the fullest development of Jewish ritual, such as we find it in the Book of Leviticus, was directly due in a great measure

to the ceremonial ideals sketched out by Ezekiel in the last portion of his book, chs. xl.-xlviii.

On the other hand, we find in the prophets frequent protests against mere formalism, and even hints that certain outward forms of religion were neither absolutely necessary, nor intended to be of permanent obligation. Thus Jeremiah speaks of a time when "they shall say no more, The ark of the covenant of Yahweh: neither shall it come to mind: neither shall they remember it; neither shall they visit it; neither shall it be made any more" (iii. 16). There can be little doubt that Jeremiah here puts the ark for the whole system of ritual worship of which it was the centre. The passage reminds us of the indignant protest of the same prophet against those who said, "The temple of Yahweh, the temple of Yahweh, the temple of Yahweh, are these" (vii. 4). Again, Jeremiah prepares the way for St Paul's teaching concerning the true circumcision of the heart: "Circumcise yourselves to Yahweh, and take away the foreskins of your heart, ye men of Judah and inhabitants of Jerusalem: lest My fury go forth like fire, and burn that none can quench it, because of the evils of your doings" (iv. 4). The Deutero-Isaiah speaks of the great World-Temple of God, and declares that sacrifices without contrition of heart are no better than idolatry and murder: "Thus saith Yahweh, The heaven is My throne, and the earth is My footstool: what manner of house will ye build unto Me? and what place shall be My rest? For all these things hath

Mine hand made, and so all these things came to be, saith Yahweh : but to this man will I look, even to him that is poor and of a contrite spirit, and that trembleth at My word. He that killeth an ox is as he that slayeth a man ; he that sacrificeth a lamb as he that breaketh a dog's neck ; he that offereth an oblation, as he that offereth swine's blood ; he that burneth frankincense, as he that blesseth an idol " (Isa. lxvi. 1-3). In another passage he speaks of the whole nation as priests (lxi. 6). Somewhat similarly the writer of the last chapters of Zechariah, directly after he has said that all nations would be compelled to come up year by year to keep the Feast of Tabernacles, says that in that day the bells of the horses would be as holy as the high priest's dress, and every pot in Jerusalem as holy as the bowls used in the sacred ritual (xiv. 20, 21).

How, then, are we to explain this inconsistency in the utterances of the Jewish prophets, sometimes speaking as though the sacrificial system would be permanent, and even of greater importance than heretofore, at other times as about to be abolished in the great future, or to be so transformed that the people would become a universal priesthood in a universal temple ? If such a passage as the last referred to stood alone, we might answer the question by saying that the observance of the Feast of Tabernacles is merely a symbolical figure for the unity of the nations in one religion, emanating from Jerusalem. But in most of the passages quoted there is not the least reason to suppose that any but the literal meaning is intended. The true solution seems to be that while the prophets, generally speaking, contemplated as a fact the continuance of the sacrificial system, they wished to emphasise the infinitely greater importance of the spiritual side of religion.

(4) We now pass on to consider the other great religious institution of the Jews—the prophets. Here again we find the same apparent inconsistency. Isaiah foretells more than once that, in the great future, the religious teachers of the people are no longer to be dishonoured and disregarded. In chap. xxix. he compares the condition of prophecy, as it then was, to a sealed book, which some cannot read because it is sealed, and others because they are unlearned; but foretells a time when the teaching would have such a penetrating force, that even the deaf would hear the words of the book, and the eyes of the blind see out of obscurity (xxix. 11-13, 18). A similar promise is less emphatically made in the following chapter: "And though Yahweh give you the bread of adversity, and the water of affliction, yet shall not thy teachers be hidden any more, but thine eyes shall see thy teachers: and thine ears shall hear a word behind thee, saying, This is the way, walk ye in it, when ye turn to the right hand, and when ye turn to the left" (xxx. 20, 21). Jeremiah, too, promises that God will provide shepherds according to His own heart, who will feed the people with knowledge and understanding" (iii. 15; see also xxiii. 4). On the other hand, we find

the writer of Zech. xiii. foretelling a time when the prophetic office will be utterly in disrepute: " And it shall come to pass in that day, saith Yahweh of hosts, that . . . I will cause the prophets and the unclean spirit to pass out of the land. And it shall come to pass that, when any shall yet prophesy, then his father and his mother that begat him shall say unto him, Thou shalt not live; for thou speakest lies in the name of Yahweh: and his father and his mother that begat him shall thrust him through when he prophesieth. And it shall come to pass in that day, that the prophets shall be ashamed every one of his vision, when he prophesieth; neither shall they wear a hairy mantle to deceive: but he shall say, I am no prophet, I am a tiller of the ground; for I have been made a bondman from my youth. And one shall say unto him, What are these wounds between thine arms? Then he shall answer, Those with which I was wounded in the house of my friends" (2-6). That is to say, rather than have his self-mutilations recognised as the marks of a prophet, he would pretend to have been the victim of some drunken brawl. It may be objected that the writer here has in his mind the false prophets. This is true in a certain sense. But there can be little doubt that at this time the term "false prophets" would have included, at least in the view of such a writer as Jeremiah (who was probably a contemporary of this prophet), the great class of official prophets, the members of those prophetic guilds which had certainly existed from the time of Elijah and Elisha. This order had become so corrupt and full of hypocrisy, that in the time to come people would rise up in rebellion against it, and both the office and the name would disappear (*cf.* xxiii. 33-40).

And so the way is prepared for the higher thought, that just as the people were to be all priests, so they were to be all prophets. We have a familiar example of this in the promise of the New Covenant given by Jeremiah: "This is the covenant that I will make with the house of Israel after those days, saith Yahweh; I will put My law in their inward parts, and in their heart will I write it; and I will be their God, and they shall be My people: and they shall teach no more every man his neighbour, and every man his brother, saying, Know the Lord: for they shall all know Me, from the least of them unto the greatest of them, saith Yahweh" (xxxi. 33, 34). But the thought is most developed in the great prophecy of Joel: "And it shall come to pass afterward, that I will pour out My spirit upon all flesh: and your sons and your daughters shall prophesy, your old men shall dream dreams, your young men shall see visions: and also upon the servants and upon the handmaids in those days will I pour out My spirit" (ii. 28, 29). This indwelling of the Spirit is also a favourite thought of Ezekiel: "A new heart also will I give you, and a new spirit will I put within you: and I will take away the stony heart out of your flesh, and I will give you an heart of flesh. And I will put My spirit within you, and cause you to walk in My statutes, and ye shall keep My judgments and do them" (xxxvi. 26, 27). It is a significant fact that to these two priestly prophets we owe some of the most spiritual teaching of the Old Testament. It is surely a shallow opinion that holds that the letter must necessarily exclude the spirit. If it be asked what the prophets meant by the Spirit of God in such passages, we must answer, "At the very least it must have meant a power divine in its origin, giving man a keener insight into things spiritual, and a nobler sense of duty." Inspiration in this sense was to be, in the great future, the possession, not of a single body of teachers, but of the whole community.

II. And so we have already passed to the second branch of our subject — the inward and spiritual teaching of the prophets. To give even a complete outline of this teaching within reasonable limits is clearly impossible. All that I shall attempt, beyond what I have already said, is to point out a few of those great religious themes which bear most directly on the subject. (1). Among the religious privileges and duties of the great future most dwelt upon are the forgiveness of sins (*e.g.* Mic. vii. 18, 19), purity of life (*e.g.* Isa. iv. 3, 4), prayer (*e.g.* Zech. xiii. 9), faith in Yahweh; and following upon these (2) what we should call the *moral* qualities of truth and righteousness, but which were, to the mind of the prophets, as much part of their religion as the others. What words can express more exquisitely the strength and beauty of faith than these: "Thou wilt keep him in perfect peace, whose mind is stayed on Thee : because he trusteth in Thee. Trust ye in Yahweh for ever: for in Yah Yahweh is an everlasting rock" (xxvi. 3,4)?

The virtue on which the prophets lay the greatest stress is righteousness, and that for the very reason that injustice and oppression had been the besetting sin of the Jewish nation. Thus in Isa. xxxiii. 14-17, the sinners in Zion, terrified at God's judgment on the Assyrians, ask : "Who among us shall dwell with the devouring fire ? who among us shall dwell with everlasting burnings ?" The answer given is, "He that walketh righteously, and speaketh uprightly; he that despiseth the gain of oppressions, that shaketh his hands from holding of bribes, that stoppeth his ears from hearing of blood, and shutteth his eyes from looking upon evil; he shall dwell on high : his place of defence shall be the munitions of rocks: his bread shall be given him ; his waters shall be sure. Thine eyes shall see the King in His beauty : they shall behold a far-stretching land." I need hardly call to mind the similar language of the fifteenth psalm, which I have quoted at the beginning of this chapter, (*cf.* also Zeph. iii. 13). Zechariah again thus speaks of the flying roll (by which is signified God's curse): "It shall enter into the house of the thief, and into the house of him that sweareth falsely by My name: and it shall abide in the midst of his house, and shall consume it with the timber thereof and the stones thereof" (v. 4). Lastly, Isaiah foretells the destruction of those "that watch for iniquity, that make a man an offender in a cause, and lay a snare for him that reproveth in the gate, and turn aside the just with a thing of nought" (xxix. 20, 21).

(3) Of still greater importance is the change of view inaugurated by the prophets respecting man's relation to God. I need not do more than mention the thought of the nearness of God to His people in the great future, as I shall have occasion to speak of it more fully in a later chapter. What I would now call attention to is the sense of God's fatherhood, and of His unbounded love, which was to mark the new religious era. This thought is very prominent in the great prophecy of the Deutero-Isaiah. Let me illustrate it by a passage, which speaks with an eloquence unparalleled perhaps in Old Testament literature: "Seek ye Yahweh while He may be found, call ye upon Him while He is near: let the wicked forsake his way, and the unrighteous man his thoughts: and let him return unto Yahweh, and He will have mercy upon him: and to our God, for He will abundantly pardon. For My thoughts are not your thoughts, neither are your ways My ways, saith Yahweh. For as the heavens are higher than the earth, so are My ways higher than your ways, and My thoughts than your thoughts" (lv. 6-9). And in chap. lxiii. the prophet shews how this new sense of God's love explains all the difficulties of God's dealings with His people in the past. He had loved them as children from the very first: "In His love and in His pity He redeemed them; and He bare them, and carried them

all the days of old. But they rebelled, and grieved His Holy Spirit: therefore He was turned to be their enemy, and Himself fought against them" (lxiii. 9, 10). But for all that He could never be anything else but a Father, and so the people could appeal once again to His love: "Look down from heaven, and behold from the habitation of Thy holiness and of Thy glory: where is Thy zeal and Thy mighty acts? the yearning of Thy bowels and Thy compassions are restrained toward me. For Thou art our Father, though Abraham knoweth us not, and Israel doth not acknowledge us: Thou, Yahweh, art our Father; our Redeemer from everlasting is Thy name."[1]

It is just in such, to us commonplace, religious ideas that the great value of the prophets lies, not only intrinsically, but for the Christian apologist. We are so familiar with thoughts like these in the New Testament, and in religious literature of all kinds, that we expect them, as a matter of course, in all the books of the Bible. When we find them in the prophets, therefore, they do not strike us, and we often fail to realise how far advanced the prophets must have been beyond the ideas and feelings of their own times. The real wonder, if we could but see it, is that they were able to anticipate so much of the religion of Christianity. And yet it is no wonder, after all, to him who not only holds it as a pious opinion, but sees in the prophets, by his own study of their books, that they were moved by the Holy Spirit to prepare the way for the teaching of Christ.

[1] *Ibid.* 15, 16.

CHAPTER VII

THE MESSIANIC KING

"Rejoice greatly, O daughter of Zion; shout, O daughter of Jerusalem: behold, thy King cometh unto thee."—ZECH. ix. 9.

IN the last two chapters I pointed out some of the more general features of the great Future to which the prophets were continually directing the aspirations of the Jewish people. These prophetic pictures are most of them only so far Messianic that they came to be associated more or less definitely with the expectation of a unique Personality. But there is another much smaller group of prophecies in which such a Being appears as the central figure of the picture. I now wish to point out what the prophets have to say of this Figure, and how the idea of the Messiah shaped itself in the national consciousness.

It might be supposed that all that is necessary is to collect a few familiar passages out of the Psalms and Prophets, which describe what is generally understood to be some one or other characteristic of the future Messiah. But once more it must be said that such a method is to the student of historical theology apt to be very misleading. We are in danger of arguing backwards instead of forwards; of assuming, without proof, the existence throughout the course of Jewish history, of a complete and familiar Messianic idea, to which the several passages are but references; whereas, in all probability, they are but evidence of many several germs of thought out of which the idea of the Messiah grew. This will become clearer as we endeavour to trace this growth in outline.

But there may be some who object to the thought of growth in connexion with any matter of revelation, or at the most they would admit the thought only in this sense—that God gave fuller knowledge of His will, as men became better able, morally and intellectually, to grasp it; in the same way that we teach children gradually, as their improving faculties make them better able to learn. But this analogy, if really admissible, gives us all that we are arguing for. It is true that we impart to children higher knowledge, as they become more capable of digesting it; but, after all, the real advance and progress is in the power which the child acquires, not merely of imbibing ready-made ideas, but of adapting them and of developing them for himself. In all thorough education it is impossible to draw a sharp line between the ideas put into a child's mind by others and those formed or remodelled by the child himself. And if this is true of our imperfect efforts in education, why should it not be true of God's education of the Jewish people? We may feel certain that the growth of theological ideas among the Jews, more than among any other ancient people, was under divine guidance, and contained a divine element; but we may be quite incapable of saying how far any one religious idea was the product of human reason or imagination, and how far it was due to the direct agency of God's Holy Spirit. We know, for example, that, according to a very ancient tradition, Abraham at one time of his life conceived an intense desire to offer up to God what was best and dearest to him. We may have little difficulty in believing that this desire was a direct inspiration of God. But we may find it very difficult to feel sure in what exact degree the form which this desire took differed essentially from the child-sacrifices common among many primitive peoples.[1] And what is true of inspired impulses is still more likely to be true of inspired thoughts. I have already pointed out in an earlier chapter that the predictions of ordinary historical events had undoubtedly elements of purely human expectation and of human imagination, and that they were not always fulfilled in detail as the prophets themselves expected, still less in the form in which their poetic fancy dressed them.[2] But if this be so, it is likely to have been also the case with their predictions of the great national hope. And yet we may find it almost impossible to draw the line between these human elements and the divine truth with which the prophets were inspired.

But at this point the objection may be raised—

[1] See Prof. Sayce's *Patriarchal Palestine*, ed. 1895, ch. iv. p. 185.
[2] See pp. 51-60.

How then can we be certain that such predictions had a divine element at all? The answers to this objection have been in a measure forestalled in earlier chapters.[1] They seem to lie mainly in the religious and moral tone of the prophets; but partly also in the fact that their predictions of historical events were fulfilled in a degree which cannot be accounted for readily on purely natural grounds. These two arguments will probably appeal with different force to different minds; but the first will only be seen in its full force by those who have kindled their lamp from the prophet's fire. If the Hebrew prophets were not the mere "soothsayers like the Philistines" of whom Isaiah spoke with such honest contempt (ii. 6), they were something infinitely better—the giant-champions of religion, righteousness, and purity, handing down to future ages an ideal of religious and social life towards which the religious world is even now still striving.

But if we cannot with perfect certainty distinguish the divine and human elements, we can at least gather together these great thoughts of the future as they unfolded themselves in successive ages, and then shew to what extent and with what limitations they were fulfilled in Christianity. It will be my aim, then, in this and the next two chapters, to point out and illustrate some of the great thoughts which culminated in the Messianic hope. For let us bear in mind that this hope came, more or less definitely, to be the

---

[1] See chs. ii., iii.

possession of the whole Jewish people. It was in its leading traits, at any rate, no afterthought of Christianity. It forms a prominent element in the great mass of Jewish literature. That this hope belonged to different classes of Jews in the time of Christ is abundantly evident from the New Testament, and it cannot be seriously doubted that Christ based His claims to belief on the ground that He was the long-expected Messiah.

Now it is undoubtedly under the aspects of an anointed king that the Messianic hope most frequently presents itself. The frequent attempts on the part of the people to make Jesus a king, the accusations of treason against Him for rebelling against Cæsar, shew how closely connected this idea of kingship was with the thought of the Messiah. If we try to trace this idea to its source, we shall find that it originated in the conception of Theocracy. God Himself was the real King of the Jewish people. The earthly king was merely His deputy.

Possibly we may trace this theocratic idea still further up to a tendency common among ancient Eastern peoples to regard their sovereign as a sort of human deity. The lately-discovered Tel-el-Amarna tablets shew us to what lengths this notion was sometimes carried. We there see that the common formula, in which the king of Egypt was addressed by the petty kings of Palestine, in the century before the Exodus, was—" To the king my lord, my god, my sun-god, seven times seven do I prostrate myself . . . thy servant, the dust of thy feet."[1] That this is not meant as an imaginary act of homage to the gods of Egypt in addition to the king is clear from the language of the despatches, in which the acts of the Egyptian king are expressly described as the acts of a god. For example, in the despatch of the king of Simyra, an ancient city of Phœnicia, we meet with the following sentence: "but the god (even the king) heard the words of the servant of his justice, and the god brought life to his servant, and he inquired into the action of his servant a second time." In another clause of the same despatch the Egyptian king is called "the god of heaven and earth." In another despatch he is called both the Sun-god and the son of the Sun-god. This despatch is short and very characteristic. It runs as follows: "To the king my lord, my god, my Sun-god, the Sun-god who (rises) from the divine heaven is his name! Pitya, of the city of Ashkelon, thy servant, the dust that is beneath thy feet, the groom of thy horses; at the sole of the feet of the king my lord, seven times seven do I fall. Thou art glorious and supreme; and now I guard the place of the king, which (has been entrusted) to me, and all the despatches of the king my lord to me have been obeyed quite fully. But the Calebite has not yet obeyed the command of the king his lord, the son of the Sun-god." Such language may be regarded as in itself not much more than an extravagant form of

---

[1] This and the following quotations are taken from *Letters from Syria and Palestine*. By A. H. Sayce, M.A. Manchester, 1890.

court etiquette; but, whatever it may have come to mean, at any rate it points to an original belief that the king himself bore something of a divine character.

Among the Jews this thought was at once more refined and more reverent. The king was under the special protection of God, and acted for God upon earth. This close relationship to God was often expressed by the figure of sonship. We have noticed the occurrence of this thought in one of Tel-el-Amarna despatches, but there it is only an exception. The actual identity of the king with the Sun-god is the rule. Not so among the Jews. The promise made to David by Nathan with reference to Solomon, is that God would be his Father, and he God's son (2 Sam. vii. 14, 15), and this thought is emphasised in what is apparently said of a Jewish king in Ps. ii.: "Thou art my son; this day have I begotten thee." God, as the Lord of all the earth, gives His Son a right to possess even "the uttermost parts of the earth." And, if the first clause of the last verse is genuine, the nations can only appease the anger of God by paying homage to His Son. "Kiss the Son, lest He be angry, and ye perish in the way. For His wrath will soon be kindled." [1]

[1] The genuineness of this clause is, however, very uncertain. The chief difficulty is that, while the psalm as a whole is a specimen of the best classical Hebrew, the first two words of this verse are Aramaic. If they are genuine, we shall have to place the date of the psalm very late, whereas both style and ;contents point to a time, at any rate anterior to the Exile. The position of the psalm does not in this case help us. Though it occurs in the first book, which was probably the earliest collection of psalms, it probably was not there originally, for,

In the passage of 2 Samuel, already referred to, the thought is more spiritual. What the writer emphasises is the loving care and tenderness of God for His Son. "If he commit iniquity, I will chasten him with the rod of men, and with the stripes of the children of men. But My mercy shall not depart from him, as I took it from Saul, whom I put away before thee. And thine house and thy kingdom shall be made secure for ever before thee: thy throne shall be established for ever." This double thought, the love of God to His kingly son, both in mercy and in correction, is beautifully expanded and commented upon by the Exilic or post-Exilic writer of Ps. lxxxix. The promise made to David is more definitely explained as extending to the royal line in perpetuity. "His seed also will I make to endure for ever, and his throne as the days of heaven" (29). But history had not apparently justified such a promise. The city had been destroyed, the people carried away captive. King and people alike were the scorn of their mighty heathen neighbours. Yet faith would not allow the Psalmist to despair. All this misfortune might be an

like the first psalm, it has no title. In all probability it was added as an introduction to the first Book, just as the first was added at a far later period to form an introduction to the whole Psalter. On the whole, it seems probable that it belongs to the eighth or the seventh century, and that the words in question are a later gloss, taking the place, probably, of some illegible words. This would account for the peculiar readings of the versions, δράξασθε παιδείας (lxx.), etc., which cannot have been intended as a paraphrase of the Aramaic words. But if so, the latter must have been added after the lxx. translation was made, and can therefore be hardly earlier than the second century.

instance of God's corrective discipline. And so identifying himself with his people, he makes one passionate appeal to God's ancient promise. "How long, Yahweh, wilt Thou hide Thyself for ever? How long shall Thy wrath burn like fire? O remember how short my time is: For what vanity hast Thou created all the children of men! ... Yahweh, where are Thy former mercies, which Thou swarest unto David in Thy faithfulness. Remember, Yahweh, the reproach of Thy servants; how I do bear in my bosom the reproach of all the mighty peoples; wherewith thine enemies have reproached, O Yahweh; wherewith they have reproached the footsteps of Thine anointed" (Ps. lxxxix. 46-51. Cf. also Ps. cxxxii. 11, 12; Isa. lv. 3). In this and other passages of the kind we see a clear distinction between a glorious vision of a monarch fulfilling the theocratic idea of divine sonship at the head of a righteous and God-loving people, and the actual condition of things in which both prince and nation were suffering for their past sins.

But did the prophets and psalmists foresee a single Person, who would realise this idea, or did they contemplate a succession of such kings as they describe? In all probability it was generally the latter. The apparently individual and personal character of the description was the inevitable result of the form in which the prophetic prediction is generally cast. Their method was to draw pictures of a future scene, rather than to foretell future events. Thus a single king may be actually described, where a succession of kings is really intended. In at least one very remarkable instance we can prove this to have been so. In Jer. xxiii. we have the well-known passage in which the prophet foretells the springing up of a shoot from the fallen trunk of David's house, the righteous King, whose advent Jeremiah expected in close connexion with the Return from the Captivity. "Behold, the days come, saith Yahweh, that I will raise unto David a righteous Shoot, and he shall reign as king and deal wisely, and shall execute judgment and justice in the land. In his days Judah shall be saved, and Israel shall dwell safely: and this is his name whereby he shall be called, Yahweh is our righteousness" (xxiii. 5, 6). If this passage stood alone, we should certainly have supposed that Jeremiah is predicting an individual monarch. But in ch. xxxiii. 14, 15, the prophecy is repeated, and these words are added by way of explanation. "For thus saith Yahweh, David shall never want a man to sit upon the throne of the house of Israel; neither shall the priests the Levites want a man before me to offer burnt offerings, and to burn meal offerings, and to do sacrifice continually" (xxxiii. 17, 18). From this it would seem evident that Jeremiah himself contemplated a succession of kings and a succession of priests.

But the genuineness of the whole section (vv. 14-26) has been much disputed, partly because of its omission by the LXX. and partly because it assumes a more priestly tone than Jeremiah generally adopts.

It is, however, quite possible that the first may have arisen through the attempt of the LXX., or more probably some earlier scribes, to revise the order.[1] Its similarity to the earlier prophecy may have caused it by some rearrangement of this kind to slip out of the text. As to the second objection, it must be borne in mind that Jeremiah took his start, so to speak, from a religious Reformation inaugurated by the Priests; and he was certainly not wanting in priestly sympathies. But, whatever view we take of this passage, one thing is perfectly clear: The writer is here avowedly explaining and expanding the prophecy of ch. xxiii. He now declares that the prophecy would be fulfilled (a) in connexion with the return from the Captivity, (b) by a restoration of the royal line of David, (c) by a rehabilitation of the priesthood also. There is nothing to imply that the High Priest is put on a level with the King, or indeed that a High Priest, in the Levitical sense of the word, is contemplated. There are, however, many points which connect this section with Jeremiah. For example, the promise in vv. 17, 18, with its characteristic phrase, "shall never want a man," recalls the similar promise to Jonadab, the son of Rechab, in xxxv. 19. Again, the identification of the Priests and Levites in vv. 18-22

---

[1] Traces of this revision appear even in the earlier prophecies, in xxiii., where 7, 8, have been transposed to the end of the chapter, but it was only completely carried out in chapters xlvi.-li. It seems obvious that the translators could not have written $\mathrm{'Ιωσεδὲκ\ ἐν\ τ.\ προφήταις}$ in xxiii. 6, 9, unless they had found vv. 7, 8 *already* transposed from this place.

is just what we should expect in Jeremiah's time, when the Levites had not yet been degraded from the priestly rank and made to perform menial offices, *cf.* Deut. xvii. 9, xxiv. 8 with Ezek. xliv. 10-14. Putting these two facts together, we may say that, even if Jeremiah did not write the section, the passage shews what interpretation was put upon Jeremiah's prophecy of ch. xxiii. by one who belonged to his school, and was almost his contemporary.

Even if the prophets did not in every case, and possibly did not in any case, predict a single Messianic King, they at least prepared the way for the thought. A perfect Ideal suggested a perfect Being who should fulfil the Ideal. And thus, if not by direct prophetic prediction, we find that the hope of a single Messianic King became deeply rooted in the heart of the Jewish people. In one passage at least (Zech. xii. 8) the future King is compared to the Angelic Representative of God, who is said to have led the Israelites in the wilderness. "In that day will Yahweh defend the inhabitants of Jerusalem; and he that is feeble among them at that day shall be as David; and the house of David shall be as God, as the angel of Yahweh before them." I need not remind students of the Hexateuch that "the angel of Yahweh" is described as no ordinary angel, but as a personal embodiment of the Divine Being Himself (see, *e.g.*, Ex. xxiii. 21; Numb. xxii. 23-36). If a large number of commentators are right in saying that what is said of the angel of Yahweh is a feeling after the doctrine of the Incarnation, then we shall be justified in regarding this as one of the most striking predictions of the God-King. It is important, however, to bear in mind that even here the words " House of David " seem to point to a succession of God-like kings.

But the language of the unique prophecy of Isaiah ix. is bolder still. It cannot be seriously doubted that the words, " The mighty God, the everlasting Father," are intended for actual titles of the King. So completely did this King on earth represent Almighty God, that some of the highest titles of God could be given to Him. The words " everlasting Father " have proved to some a very serious theological difficulty. But what reason have we to expect in Isaiah the theological exactness of the Nicene Council? The use of the word " Father " at all, had Isaiah intended by it to express the relation of God the Father to the eternal Son, would have been indeed a strange anachronism. But what word could more forcibly and tenderly express that almighty love of God, which would be seen in the Person and actions of the Great King? In contemplating the Ideal King, the prophet is inspired with thoughts which in their completeness could only be realised in an Incarnate God.

A far more common conception is that Yahweh would take the place of the earthly king. This is especially frequent in the last period of the Jewish monarchy, when the weak and worldly character of the kings made the prophets at times give up all hopes of the Davidic family. In the passage already discussed Jeremiah foretells the perpetuity of the Davidic kings and of the Levitic priests, (xxxiii. 17-18). This, if in its true place, was written during the siege of Jerusalem. But at an earlier period he speaks in a different tone. In iii. 16-17, he foretells a time when the presence of God as King would supersede not only the kingdom, but apparently the priesthood also. "And it shall come to pass, when ye be multiplied and increased in the land, in those days, saith Yahweh, they shall say no more, The ark of the covenant of Yahweh, neither shall it come to mind: neither shall they remember it; neither shall they visit it; neither shall it be made any more. At that time they shall call Jerusalem the throne of Yahweh; and all the nations shall be gathered unto it, to the name of Yahweh, to Jerusalem." We find the same thought in the probably contemporary writer of Zechariah xiv.,[1] who speaks of a time when the remnant of all nations would be compelled to go up every year to Jerusalem to worship the King, Yahweh of hosts, (16-17).

I have hitherto spoken of the personality of the King. Let us now see what the prophets have to say of his work and character. We find him described frequently as a mighty conqueror subduing his enemies on all hands, and bringing distant countries under his authority. I have already referred to Psalm ii. But, perhaps, the most typical instance is

[1] Some critics, however, put the prophecy much later.

in the so-called psalm of Solomon, "He shall have dominion also from sea to sea, and from the River unto the ends of the earth. They that dwell in the wilderness shall bow before him; and his enemies shall lick the dust. The kings of Tarshish and of the isles shall bring presents; the kings of Sheba and Seba shall offer gifts. Yea, all kings shall fall down before him; all nations shall serve him." (Ps. lxxii. 8-11). It may be objected that such psalms are not predictions of a future king, but descriptions of one who was actually reigning at the time. This is probably true in many cases, but it is equally true that the descriptions which the psalmists give did not yet apply to the reigning sovereign, but rather to the ideal of sovereignty for which they were hoping and praying, an ideal thrown farther and farther into the future as king after king failed to realise it.

Again, the reign of the King was to be a reign of peace and security under divine protection. Isaiah, in ix., calls the king a prince of peace, and speaks of the soldiers' clothes and boots being burnt for fuel of fire. Similarly in Zech. ix. a prophet predicts a time when God would "cut off the chariot from Ephraim and the horse from Jerusalem, and the battle-bow" would be "cut off, and the king" would "speak peace unto the nations." In this last passage the king's character and habits are described as a return to the simplicity of primitive times. He is to be "lowly and riding upon an ass." (9; *cf.* Judg. v. 10, x. 4, xii. 14).

Above all, the rule of the King is to be distinguished by perfect equity and perfect kindness. In the seventy-second psalm we have a beautiful description of the king's government. "For he shall deliver the needy when he crieth; the poor that hath no helper. He shall have pity on the poor and needy, and the souls of the needy he shall save. He shall redeem their soul from oppression and violence: and precious shall their blood be in his sight" (12-14). So gentle and beneficent are his words and actions that they are like the "rain upon the mown grass: as showers that water the earth" (6). And from them would spring up a fruitful crop of righteousness and peace. But the most complete description of the King is that of Isa. xi. 1-5, where gentleness and power, wisdom and justice are like the four notes of an exquisitely harmonious chord.

A Sovereign divine in power, divine in wisdom, divine in love and justice, mighty to conquer and mighty to save. Such was the vision of the prophets and psalmists, a vision seen but dimly *even by them* through the earthly halo in which their imagination clothed it. Can we altogether wonder if the Jewish people failed to recognise the object of prophetic vision in the lowly greatness of the Carpenter of Nazareth?

CHAPTER VIII

THE PROPHETIC AND PRIESTLY ASPECTS OF THE MESSIAH

"Thus speaketh Yahweh of hosts, saying, Behold the man whose name is the Shoot; and He shall shoot up out of His place, and He shall build the temple of Yahweh, even He shall build the temple of Yahweh; and He shall bear the glory, and shall sit and rule upon His throne; and He shall be a priest upon His throne: and the counsel of peace shall be between them both."—ZECH. vi. 12, 13.

WE are accustomed to think of the Messiah under the three aspects of Prophet, Priest, and King. The third of these I have already discussed in the last chapter. The first two I wish to speak of in this. Of the prophetic office of the Messiah little need be said. I doubt, indeed, whether, properly speaking, it belongs to my subject at all. There is only one prophecy in the Old Testament which definitely predicts, or seems to definitely predict, the Messiah in the character of a prophet. I refer, of course, to the well-known prediction of Deut. xviii. 15, ff. "Yahweh thy God will raise up unto thee a Prophet from the midst of thee, of thy brethren, like unto Me," etc. But, except perhaps among the Samaritans,[1] there is no proof that this prophecy was ever, before the founding of Christianity, interpreted of the Messiah.

[1] See John iv. 25-29.

It is no doubt true that Jesus was known as the "Prophet from Nazareth" (Matt. xxi. 11), and admitted the applicability of the title "Prophet" to Himself (St Luke iv. 24). But it is not the fact itself which is in question. No one can doubt that a large number of Jews recognised in Christ a very exceptional teacher, a prophet in at least the New Testament sense of the word. Some of them also believed him to be the Messiah. But there is nothing to shew that, like the Samaritan woman, they thought Him at all more likely to be the Messiah because he was a prophet.

It is also true, of course, that the Jewish people in the time of Christ expected the appearance of some great prophet in connexion with the advent of the Messiah. But, as we gather from more than one passage in St John's Gospel,[1] the prophet is clearly distinguished from the Messiah Himself. This expectation seems to have originated from the prophecy in the last chapter of Malachi, which foretold the return of Elijah. The tradition that Jeremiah, and probably some other of the great prophets also, would return appears to have arisen by analogies from this. (Matt. xvi. 14). But in Malachi the work of Elijah stands in direct contrast to that of the "messenger of the covenant." The latter is to purify by chastisement the sons of Levi, as a preparation for the coming of Yahweh Himself to annihilate the wicked. "Yah-

[1] Especially i. 19-21, vii. 40-41.

weh, whom ye seek, shall suddenly come to His temple; and the messenger of the covenant, whom ye delight in, behold he cometh, saith Yahweh of hosts. But who may abide the day of His coming? and who shall stand when He appeareth? for He is like a refiner's fire, and like fullers' sope. And He shall sit as a refiner and purifier of silver, and He shall purify the sons of Levi, and purge them as gold and silver; and they shall offer unto Yahweh offerings in righteousness. . . . And I will come near to you to judgment; and I will be a swift witness against the sorcerers, and against the adulterers, and against false-swearers, and against those that oppress the hireling in his wages, the widow and the fatherless, and that turn aside the stranger from his right, and fear not Me, saith Yahweh of hosts." But the work of Elijah is to avert this judgment by repentance. "Behold I will send you Elijah the prophet before the great and terrible day of Yahweh come. And he shall turn the heart of the fathers to the children, and the heart of the children to their fathers, lest I come and smite the earth with a curse." (Mal. iii. 1-3, 5, iv. 5-6.)

Again, if we except the doubtful passage of Deuteronomy (xviii. 15), there is none which definitely predicts a great future teacher. At any rate there arose no great prophetic ideal at all comparable with the kingly ideal of which I spoke in the last chapter. Even where prophets are foretold in the new order of things, little stress is laid on their personality and office.[1] The office of the Messianic King is to conquer, to rule, to judge, but not to teach. We may say, of course, that Christ, as a fact, fulfilled the prophecy of Deuteronomy more completely than any one of the great prophets, Jeremiah for example; but we cannot say that the prophetic character was part of the current conception of the Messiah, as foretold by the prophets, and expected by the Jewish people.

It has, however, been maintained [2] that in the time of the Maccabees at any rate the Messianic hope of the Jewish nation was directed towards a prophet. This view is based on two passages, 1 Mac. iv. 46 and xiv. 41. The first occurs in the description of the cleansing of the sanctuary after its pollution by Antiochus Epiphanes. The question arose, What should be done with the desecrated altar? The priests finally determined to pull it down, and lay up the stones "in the mountain of the temple in a convenient place, until there should come a prophet to shew what should be done with them." This only proves that at that time there was a hope that the prophetic order, which had long been in abeyance, would be again restored. The second passage (xiv. 41) is perhaps more to the point. The writer is giving a very full and laudatory account of Simon the Maccabee. He says that "the Jews and priests were well pleased that Simon should be their high priest for ever, until

---

[1] See above, p. 110, ff.
[2] As *e.g.* by Prof. Cheyne, Bampton Lectures, p. 20.

there should arise a faithful prophet." But even this need mean nothing more than that the priests, or perhaps one should say rather the writer himself, felt that any decision of theirs might be overruled if a really trustworthy prophet should arise. Even if such passages, taken in connexion with those already referred to, justify us in supposing that there did exist among the Jews at times the hope of a Messianic Prophet, this conception was, as it were, spasmodic and altogether independent of the constant hope of the Messianic King.

The same cannot be said of the priestly conception of the Messiah. Though not, it is true, from the first a characteristic of the Coming One, it appears very definitely at that stage in the history of prophecy, which followed the Return from the Captivity. This period was marked by the increased importance which was attached to all connected with the ritual worship of the temple. And, as a result of this, far greater reverence came to be felt for the priests, and especially the high priest. Some commentators have seen in the writings of this period evidence of an antagonistic rivalry between the princely representatives of the royal house and the high priest. At any rate we do certainly find by the side of the old kingly ideal, so frequent in the earlier prophets, the growth of a second ideal, the priestly. This we find reflected in the books of the two contemporary prophets, Haggai and Zechariah.

Haggai, it is true, attaches the highest importance to the princely office. For though in five cases out of the six in which he mentions Zerubbabel he couples with his name that of Joshua, the high priest, yet he invariably mentions Zerubbabel first.[1] And not only so, but in the last prophecy (ii. 20-23), which is addressed to Zerubbabel alone, he speaks of him in language which is almost Messianic. When God has overthrown all the kingdoms of the nations, "In that day, saith Yahweh of hosts, will I take thee, O Zerubbabel my servant, the son of Shealtiel, saith Yahweh, and will make thee as a signet: for I have chosen thee, saith Yahweh of hosts." The thought is that Zerubbabel will reign alone, the darling of God, while all the surrounding nations are powerless to harm.

But in Zechariah, on the other hand, far greater stress is laid comparatively on the sacred character and exalted position of the high priest. In the earlier visions, taken as a whole, the high priest and the prince seem to occupy co-ordinate positions. It is Joshua, the high priest, who is acquitted of the charges made by Satan, and stands arrayed in the robes of innocence (iii.). It is Joshua and his fellows who are typically and spiritually connected with the coming of the Shoot (iii. 8): "Hear now, O Joshua the high priest, thou and thy fellows that sit before thee: for they are men which are a sign; for behold I will bring forth My Servant the Shoot." Again, it is before Joshua (9) that the stone is laid, having upon it seven eyes and engraven by Yahweh of hosts. But something very much of the same kind is said also of Zerubbabel in the vision

---

[1] Hag. i. 1, 12, 14; ii. 2, 4.

of the golden candlestick in iv. He was to be no mere ordinary prince acting in his own strength, but was to be specially empowered by the Spirit of God: "Not by might, nor by power, but by My Spirit, saith Yahweh of Hosts" (6). And by this means all difficulties were to be overcome. "Who art thou, O great mountain? Before Zerubbabel thou shalt become a plain" (7). On the work of Zerubbabel as he stands with the plummet in his hand, the joy of all beholders, rest those seven eyes of Yahweh (10). This co-ordination of prince and high priest is still more definite in the explanation of the two olive branches given at the end of this vision: "These are the two sons of oil, that stand by Yahweh of the whole earth" (14). Zechariah here seems to see God enshrined in the temple of the world, and ministered to by the two representatives of his worshippers, the high priest and the prince. Even the prince has something of a priestly character.

But later on, in vi. 9-15, we find, or seem to find, a new departure in Zechariah's conception of the relation of the two offices. The high priest and the prince are no longer two ministers of God standing side by side with equal dignity and power; but the offices are united in one person. Or it would be truer to say that the personality of the prince is absorbed in that of the high priest. For it is Joshua, not Zerubbabel, who is the type of this priest-king. It is on his head that the crowns of gold and silver are laid (11). He is especially pointed out as the type of the Shoot (12, 13). And of the Shoot it is expressly said that he is not only to sit and rule, but also to be a Priest upon His throne.

This, at any rate, is the most natural interpretation of this passage. But it must be confessed that a large number of recent commentators have given a different explanation. They argue (1) that the crowns being more than one, were evidently intended for more than one person. They therefore propose to read in 11 "upon the head of Zerubbabel and upon the head of Joshua," and so make what according to our present text is said of the Shoot in the next verse refer to Zerubbabel. In 13 they translate, instead of "he shall be a priest upon his throne," "there shall be a priest upon his throne," *i.e.* to say, in the future the Prince was to have a Priest sitting beside him (at his right hand, if we adopt the LXX. reading,[1]) and sharing his government; and the words that follow, "and the counsel of peace shall be between them both," would mean that the two would now rule together in perfect harmony. Now, if we could be certain that this interpretation was correct, it would merely shew that Zechariah was still contemplating the co-ordination of the two offices, rather than their union in one person. We should have to look for the latter conception at a later date.

But there are grave objections to this interpretation. (1) It involves an insertion for which there is no authority whatever, whereas the text as it stands

---

[1] In all probability this reading is a gloss from Ps. cx. 1.

is certainly quite translatable. (2) It creates as many difficulties as it removes. After saying, in 11, "Make crowns and set them upon the head of Joshua," etc., the writer continues in 12, "And speak unto *him*," *i.e.* obviously to Joshua, as the text stands. But if we make the supposed insertion in the previous verse, and read, "Place them upon the head of Zerubbabel and upon the head of Joshua," to whom do the words "unto him" refer? The commentators I speak of understand them as referring to Zerubbabel. But on grammatical grounds they may just as well, if not better, refer to Joshua; and surely the writer would have avoided this ambiguity, and repeated the name of the person signified. Again, if Zerubbabel is here the type of the coming Royal Shoot, it should have been made equally clear that Joshua is the type of the coming High Priest. For this is *ex hypothesi* the sole meaning of their coronation. But the words, "There shall be a priest upon his throne" would not suggest any connexion whatever between Joshua and the future High Priest. (3) It is also worth noticing that if we adopt the amended reading of 13, we should naturally suppose from the order that the silver crown was for Zerubbabel, the gold for Joshua, thus giving in this respect the greater honour to Joshua, who otherwise holds, according to this interpretation, a somewhat subordinate position. The only real difficulty in taking the text as it stands lies in the words, "And the counsel of peace shall be between *them both.*" But may there not be an almost unconscious reference to the existing state of things? There was then, or might be in the near future, a rivalry, if not an open antagonism, between the two offices (symbolised respectively by the gold and silver crowns); but when these two were united in one Priest-King such a thing would be impossible.

At this point an important question occurs to us. Is Zechariah here speaking as a prophet or as a politician? Is he foretelling a Messiah, or is he propounding a new scheme of government? Is he describing the priestly character of the Coming King, or merely arguing that it would be desirable in the cause of religion, and therefore for the highest welfare of his people, that they should be under the rule of the High Priest? But are we right at all in so sharply dividing these two alternatives? The vision of the Messianic King, as foreseen by the earlier prophets, Isaiah for instance, was in one sense ideal, for it was the rule of one who would perfectly fulfil the conception of theocracy — God's viceregent on earth, a perfect King ruling a perfect people. But they looked forward to this ideal, not as a pleasant dream, but as an actual possibility, something to be striven for, and they saw in the events of their own day God working for this end. To say, then, that Zechariah's prophecies deal with an ideal future, or an expected Messiah, is not to remove them, to use a modern phrase, out of the sphere of practical politics. He may not have thought that the ideal High Priest, the spiritual Head of the nation, free from all the corruptions of the past, would actually be seen in his own day, but he put forth the idea as what should be the religious aim of the nation. One thing, at any rate, is evident, that by giving the name Branch or Shoot to the person who was to fulfil his ideal, he was appealing to the Messianic hopes already raised in the people by Jeremiah (xxiii. 5). This is all the more significant when we remember that this name was given by Jeremiah, to signify that the Messiah was to shoot up from the fallen tree of the house of David. But no such idea is suggested by Zechariah's explanation of the name; he merely says, "He shall shoot up from His place" (vi. 12). In his view the Shoot is connected, not with the royal house of David, but with the high priesthood. But there is no ground for supposing that he contemplated any change in the family of the high priest.

The state of things which Zechariah foretold began to be fulfilled in its outward aspect soon after his own time. We hear of no representative of David's house succeeding to Zerubbabel; whereas the secular power passed more and more into the hands of the priests. It is true, of course, that in such a high priest as Eliashib, who proved so troublesome a thorn in Nehemiah's side, we have a person very different from Zechariah's ideal; but, in spite of such exceptions, the high priesthood came in time to be the greatest spiritual and temporal influence in the community. This power reached its climax in the person of Simon the Just, who was regarded by the Jewish people with a veneration such as no high priest either before or after could command. In Ecclus. l. 5-12 we have a beautiful description of the impression which he made as he officiated in his priestly vestments: "How was he honoured in the midst of the people in his coming out of the sanctuary! He was as the morning star in the midst of a cloud, and as the moon at the full: as the sun shining upon the temple of the Most High, and as the rainbow giving light in the bright clouds: and as the flower of roses in the spring of the year, as lilies by the rivers of waters, and as the branches of the frankincense tree in the time of summer: as fire and incense in the censer, and as a vessel of beaten gold set with all manner of precious stones: and as a fair olive tree budding forth fruit, and as a cypress tree which groweth up to the clouds. When he put on the robe of honour and was clothed with the perfection of glory, when he went up to the holy altar, he made the garment of holiness honourable, when he took the portions out of the priests' hands, he himself stood by the hearth of the altar, compassed with his brethren round about, as a young cedar in Libanus, and as palm trees compassed they him round about." But Simon was not only an honoured high priest, he was also a man of action and a great public benefactor. He restored the temple, and rebuilt the city walls, which had been demolished by Ptolemy I. (Soter). He was also one of the most celebrated of Jewish teachers. Later on the great Judas Maccabæus, and his scarcely less heroic brothers, were men of Aaronic descent, and the youngest of them, Simon II., ruled the nation as high priest. He completed the work of deliverance from Syria, which his brothers had devoted their lives to achieving, and even if he did not actually receive the *title* of king,[1] he had the reality far more than the titular Judæan kings of a later date.

There is another passage in the Old Testament, which, if not perhaps more important in itself than the prophecies of Zechariah, is at any rate more familiar. In thinking of the priestly character of the Messiah we naturally turn our thoughts to Ps. cx., and the use made of that psalm in the Epistle to the Hebrews. But there is a great difference between a psalm of this kind and a prophecy. The purpose of the latter is to picture a future ideal towards which the nation should aim; the purpose of a psalm such as this is to celebrate some person or event. The psalm is only prophetic in so far as the poet, in describing the present or the past, paints an idealised picture which is only true of some greater future. Thus it is most natural to suppose that in the second psalm the writer intends to celebrate the victory of some living king over his enemies,[2] but in doing so he represents the king as standing in an ideal relationship

---

[1] The first high priest who bore the title of king appears to have been Aristobulus (see Graetz, *Hist. of the Jews*, Eng. transl. ii. p. 35). So Josephus, but Jannæus is the first on whose coins the name king occurs.

[2] Cheyne, however (see *Book of Psalms in loco*), regards this psalm as directly Messianic.

K

to God. The same is true of Ps. cx., but with this difference, that the view of this ideal relationship has changed with the time. In Ps. ii., written apparently in the time of the Jewish monarchy, the King is God's Eternal Son; in Ps. cx. He is God's Eternal Priest.

The latter psalm is conceived in the spirit of the later prophecy of Zechariah (chap. vi.). The writer shews that the rule of the high priest is no new thing, but a restoration of the ancient patriarchal system of which Melchizedek was a well-known example. The person celebrated in the psalm belongs evidently, then, to a late period of Jewish history, and recent critics have given very strong reasons for the view that the priest-king was no other than Simon the Maccabee. There was no one in Jewish history who so thoroughly combined the dignity of the high priesthood with the qualities of a noble ruler, a clever strategist, and a courageous warrior. 1 Macc. xiv. gives us a glowing description of the prosperity of the country under his rule. The language reminds us of the Messianic pictures of the prophets. And when we read (ver. 41) that the Jews and priests were well-pleased that Simon should be their high priest for ever, until there should arise a faithful prophet, we cannot but feel that the resemblance to Ps. cx. 4 can hardly be merely a coincidence. "Yahweh hath sworn, and will not repent. Thou art a Priest for ever after the order of Melchizedek."

This view has been, it is thought, confirmed by the discovery of the name Simeon in the initial letters of four consecutive verses of the psalm, making it appear to be, like several others, an acrostic.[1]

This psalm does not add much to Zechariah's conception of the Messiah, except that it blends more completely the new priestly with the old kingly element. He does not merely sit on His throne, a high-priestly ruler, nor, if we adopt the other interpretation of the passage in Zechariah, does He sit beside the King, but as a victorious warrior He crushes His enemies in all directions (2, 5-7), Still the priestly character of the Messiah is maintained in the description of the warriors who freely devote themselves to the cause of himself and their country. "Thy people offer themselves willingly in the day of Thy power: in the beauties of holiness from the womb of the morning Thou hast the dew of thy youth"; *i.e.* the young men with armour glistening like the dew resemble a great company of priests in their holy vestments. It is needless to add that the sacred character of the Maccabæan struggle gives a special point to the psalm, if it is referred to Simon. In singing His glory the evidently contemporary psalmist gives us the ideal of the Priest-King, or in other words, of the Messiah, as it existed in the middle of the second century B.C.

It need not surprise us that the writer of the Epistle to the Hebrews should have used this psalm

[1] See *Academy*, Feb., &c., 1892. The chief difficulties lie in the fact (1) that so the name is written defectively, שמען for שמעון; and (2) that it is difficult to account for the initial letters of the last three verses, א, י, and מ.

as though it were a direct prophecy of the eternal priesthood of Christ, without any reference to the typical priest-king of the psalms, whoever he may be. His treatment of the passage not only embodies the Messianic interpretation current among the Jews, but is also in exact keeping with the methods employed throughout his whole treatise.[1]

But there is a far greater difficulty presented to us in the language of our Lord in Matt. xxii. 41-46. It is not merely that He apparently sets His seal to the current Messianic interpretation of the psalm. That would be no real difficulty. For to recognise the type is not to ignore the Antitype. To see in the psalm a primary reference to Simon is not to forget that Christ more perfectly fulfilled the Messianic ideal which is there pictured. But more than this, Christ accepts the non-critical views of the age, and ascribes the psalm to David, and even founds upon this an important theological argument. It is quite useless to urge, in answer to this difficulty that criticism is a science, and must not be hampered by theological considerations. Theological considerations may be connected with the most vital truths. Suppose, for example, that we were certain that God has said that this psalm was written by David, it would be nothing short of blasphemy to doubt the fact. Again, it is hardly more satisfactory to say that Christ's words are merely an *argumentum ad hominem*, and do not necessarily

---

[1] For instance, he argues at some length that the words of Ps. xcv. 11, 'That they should not enter into My rest' can only refer to the great rest which still awaits the people of God.

imply that He Himself recognised the Davidic authorship. To say the least of it, it would be unworthy of Christ's moral dignity to argue from premises which He knew to be untrue. And, besides, we have precisely the same difficulty in certain passages in our Lord's sayings, which imply that Moses was the author of Deuteronomy [1] and in which there is no possibility of an *argumentum ad hominem*.

The most natural alternative is to suppose that our Lord's knowledge on these points was really limited by the conditions of the time in which He lived. The *mere supposition* of ignorance cannot be regarded as inadmissible, either on the grounds of Christian doctrine or of reverence, when we bear in mind that He declared Himself ignorant on a subject of great theological importance, namely, the time of His second advent. We must admit then, on Christ's own authority, that the union of the Godhead with the Manhood did not as a fact in all cases preclude His ignorance as man. It should, of course, be distinctly borne in mind that our Lord's conclusion—the superiority of the Messiah to David—does not really depend for its truth on any argument drawn from Ps. cx.

Many explanations have been suggested on theological grounds, to account for our Lord's ignorance. But, after all, is not this the most humble and reverent attitude to take?—to confess honestly that the union of an omniscient Godhead and a limited humanity in

---

[1] *E.g.* Matt. xix. 8 ; Mark x. 3.

one Person absolutely transcends our human faculties; and that we therefore cannot say *a priori* what limitations to the one nature or the other, from our point of view, that union necessarily involved. It is enough for us that there were limitations, at any rate humanly speaking, to the ἐνέργεια of the divine nature. This is abundantly evident from the Gospel record of Him who needed to grow in wisdom as well as in stature, and who, in the startling language of St Paul, " being from the beginning in the form of God, emptied Himself and took the form of a slave, being made in the likeness of men " (Phil. ii. 6, 7). What more striking example could we find of the difficulty of conceiving and representing divine truth under the limitations of human thought and human language!

CHAPTER IX

THE ATONING VICTIM

"He was wounded for our transgressions, He was bruised for our iniquities: the chastisement of our peace was upon Him; and with His stripes we are healed."—Isa. liii. 5.

I ENDEAVOURED in the last two chapters to trace briefly the conception of the Messiah, as it gradually took shape among the Jewish people. But there is one aspect of the Messiah from the Christian point of view, and that perhaps the most important of all, which I have hitherto left untouched, the innocent victim suffering for the sins of the world. Was this also foretold by the prophets? Christians have from the earliest times confidently answered "Yes." The Jews have, speaking generally, answered "No." Of course it is well known that we do find in the Talmud, and elsewhere in Jewish literature, instances of a belief in a suffering Messiah [1]; but whatever be the true explanation of this fact, the belief itself can hardly be considered as forming part of the generally accepted Messianic doctrine, at least as it existed in the time of Christ. At most it falls very short of the Christian idea of the great atoning sacrifice. Now how far, or in what sense, does this

[1] See Essay on this subject in Cheyne's *Isaiah*.

idea find a place in the prediction of the Jewish prophets? This question I will now try to answer. But it is only possible to do so fairly and honestly by an impartial examination of those passages which have been understood to foretell the sufferings of Christ. In the short limits at my disposal, I can only deal with very few of these. But I think they will be enough to establish some general conclusions, and will serve as an example of a method of exegesis capable of a much wider application.

But there is a larger question which is really involved in the immediate subject of our inquiry, and cannot wisely be separated from it, the belief of the Jews concerning the divine purpose of suffering. There was a time when they believed that suffering was inflicted by God merely as a punishment for sin. A man's or a nation's sinfulness might be measured by their temporal calamities. We have an excellent example of this view in Ps. xxxvii.: "Fret not thyself because of evil-doers," even though they seem to prosper and thou to suffer. Why not? Because God's righteousness must vindicate itself. Their good fortunes, thy ill fortunes are but temporary. "They shall soon be cut down like the grass, and wither as the green herb," and then the time will come when "the meek shall inherit the land; and shall delight themselves in the abundance of peace" (1-11). But experience must have continually given the lie to this limited view of Providence. How often it happened that the wicked prospered, and went on prospering, while the righteous suffered, and even perished altogether! The thoughtful Jew must have felt that the problem of suffering needed another solution. What tended more than anything else to enlarge his view was the great national calamity of the Exile. What seemed at the time only a crushing disaster proved in reality to be an immense educational force, moulding the Jewish character. We see this strikingly brought out in that most fascinating of Old Testament books, the Book of Job. It was, I believe, Bishop Warburton who, in his *Divine Legation of Moses*, first propounded the, in his day, most startling opinion that this book was not written by Moses, but by some unknown writer of the time of the Exile. It was in his view no record of men and women once living, but a religious allegory—Job himself being a personification of the Jewish people. In so thinking the keen-sighted bishop anticipated more than a century ago many of the results of modern criticism. At any rate, it is now pretty well agreed that Job does not belong to the historical books of the Old Testament, but to a far later group, those ethical and philosophical treatises collectively known as the Chokmah or Wisdom. Whether the book is allegorical or not, it is considered that its real value for the theological student lies not so much in the story of Job himself, as in the supposititious dialogue with his companions. The true meaning of suffering is the main theme throughout, and the conclusion gradually arrived at is this: If Job suffered more than all men, it was not because he had committed greater sins, but because God loved him more, and therefore corrected him for his good. His punishment brought about his confession of sin, and on this followed his restoration to prosperity. And yet we must feel that this book leaves something to be desired. The concluding section of the last chapter (xlii. 7-17), in which Job is compensated manifold in kind for his previous losses, is disappointing after the magnificent climax which precedes it (chs. xxxviii.-xlii. 6). We should have been better content to have left Job still poor in earthly possessions but rich in the spiritual wealth which his sufferings had brought him. And so we can sympathise, if we cannot agree, with the suggestion of at least one modern critic,[1] that the last part was added by a later writer, who tried to satisfy in this way his idea of poetic justice. But we have no necessity to adopt such a view. For we cannot reasonably expect to find the writer as yet able to rid himself entirely of the cruder ideas of the past.

When we turn to the great prophet of the Captivity, we find a still more spiritual view of suffering. There is, indeed, some resemblance in detail between the history of Job and the description of the suffering servant of Yahweh. But, as has recently been pointed out with justice, there is this essential difference between the two, that in Isa. lii. 13-liii., the affliction of the servant has a vicarious value, whereas we do not find this thought in Job. But who is the suffering servant of Isa. liii.? To some it might seem

[1] Froude, for example.

unnecessary to ask the question. The great bulk of Christian commentators, until very recent times, have seen in this description a direct prediction of Christ crucified on the cross for the sins of the world, and nothing else. Can we do so now? Not, I think, if we study the prophecy with perfectly open minds. For if so, such a sudden portraiture of the crucified Saviour would in the immediate context of the prophecy, and in the whole religious and mental atmosphere of the prophet, be quite unintelligible. And besides, such a graphic Messianic picture would present no analogies to the other great Messianic predictions of the Old Testament. For these are invariably connected most closely with the events of the time in which the prophet lived, and in many cases the prophet appears to have seen his Messiah in some person of his own day. If, then, Isa. liii. is Messianic, even so we should expect that we have here, in the first instance, a description of some contemporary Jewish martyr.

And so commentators have seen in this chapter a direct reference to the sufferings of either Josiah or Jeremiah. But neither of them at all satisfies the requirements of the prophecy. The death of Josiah was certainly most pathetic. The universal lamentation which it evoked became a proverb. There was no mourning like "the mourning of Hadadrimmon in the valley of Megiddon" (Zech. xii. 11). But by what flight of poetic imagination could the sad result of the young king's foolhardiness be called a sin-offering for the people? Or what possible meaning could be assigned to such expressions as "his visage was so marred more than any man, and his form more than the sons of men"? (Isa. lii. 14). Indeed it is obvious that nearly the whole description could not possibly refer to one who, by a sudden death, was cut off from what might have been a glorious career.

The same objections do not apply, or at any rate with at all the same force, to Jeremiah. He may be said to have suffered during a large part of his career, in a certain sense, for the sins of his people. He was the constant victim of religious persecution, and suffered many bodily injuries, and he bore them with singular meekness of spirit. In fact, he uses of himself words which seem to find an echo in this very prophecy: "I was like a gentle lamb that is led to the slaughter; and I knew not that they had devised devices against me, saying, Let us destroy the tree with the fruit thereof" (Jer. xi. 19). Lastly, if we accept the tradition of his violent death, it was true of him that "he was taken away by oppression and by judgment." But if we so interpret the prophecy, we are met with an insuperable difficulty at its close —in the glorious end which was to follow the period of suffering. "When thou shalt make his soul an offering for sin, he shall see his seed, he shall prolong his days, and the pleasure of Yahweh shall prosper in his hand . . . Therefore will I divide him a portion with the great; and he shall divide the spoil with the strong." These words might have been applied to any Jewish king in whose line were centred the prophet's hopes of a Messiah. But it is very difficult to see how we can, without altogether wresting their meaning, refer them to Jeremiah. For example, to say that prophecy would revive and flourish again after the martyrdom of Jeremiah is to put an interpretation upon the passage which the expressions used do not the least suggest. For these reasons, as well as others, it is even more certain that we cannot regard as the subject of this prophecy the writer himself.[1]

But there is another interpretation which, if to some it seems to fall short of the full meaning of the prophecy, is, at any rate, not liable to the same objections as those already discussed, that which sees in the suffering servant of Yahweh the Jewish nation itself. This interpretation is at least as old as the great Rashi, who wrote his commentary in the last half of the eleventh century, and though the Spanish school of Jews defended it and used it as a weapon against Christianity, we have no reason whatever to doubt their perfect sincerity. They certainly went far by their clear-headed, if somewhat prosaic, exposition to justify their view. Orthodox divines cannot afford to ignore such men as Kimchi and Ibn Ezra. If this interpretation is right, it will form an exact parallel to that of Job proposed by Dr Warburton. In both cases the sufferings are those

[1] Those interpretations by which the passage is referred to Abraham or one of the other patriarchs, are obviously open to even graver objections.

which the nation underwent in exile, and the prosperity which followed is the vision of post-Exilic glory which was to follow the Return.

It will be readily seen that this interpretation has many advantages, and that in the very points in which the others, speaking generally, fail. (1) It leaves the passage in agreement with the whole tenor of the so-called Deutero-Isaiah, at any rate, of that part of it which stands in obvious connexion with this prophecy. (2) The passage so interpreted has its natural place in the Book of the Restoration. For the theme of the book is its theme. (3) Above all, this interpretation gives the same meaning to the "servant of Yahweh" which the words bear almost invariably in these chapters. This expression is twice used apparently of the prophet himself, as God's messenger to His people (Isa. xliv. 26, l. 10), but elsewhere wherever, as frequently, the meaning is obvious, it is used of the nation Israel. This usage occurs especially in the chapters preceding ch. liii. Such phrases as "Hear, O Jacob, my servant," "For my servant Jacob's sake," are of common occurrence. The most important passage for our purpose is ch. xlix. Here begins that series of prophecies, sometimes called the Book of the Servant, which finds its climax in ch. liii. It is difficult to see how the servant of ch. liii. can be other than the servant of ch. xlix. But in xlix. 1-3, the servant is expressly identified as Israel. "Listen, O isles, unto me; and hearken, ye peoples, from far; Yahweh hath called me from the womb; from the bowels of my mother hath He made mention of my name. And He hath made my mouth like a sharp sword; in the shadow of His hand hath He hid me: and He hath made me a polished shaft; in His quiver hath He kept me close; and He said unto me, Thou art my servant; Israel, in whom I will be glorified." God had called Israel from the womb. From the beginning of his national existence He had destined him to be His agent in His redemptive work for himself and others. This last is the thought expressed in the fifth and sixth verses: "And now, saith Yahweh, that formed me from the womb to be His servant, to bring Jacob again to Him, and that Israel be gathered unto Him. . . . It is too light a thing that thou shouldest be My servant to raise up the tribes of Jacob, and to restore the preserved of Israel: I will also give thee for a light to the Gentiles, that thou mayest be My salvation unto the end of the earth." A difficulty has sometimes been raised that these verses make a distinction between the servant of Yahweh and the Israelitish nation.[1] But this distinction partly arises from the fact that Israel of the Captivity was only a small fraction of the Jewish nation, partly it is a distinction drawn between the idealised servant of Yahweh, Israel as he ought to be, and Israel as he was. The contrast between the ideal and the actual is brought out with the most pathetic irony in ch. xlii. 19: "Who is blind, but my servant? or deaf,

---

[1] See Cheyne's *Isaiah, in loco.*

as my messenger that I send? Who is blind as he that is at peace with me, and blind as Yahweh's servant?" Even Israel, as he was, was potentially the servant of Yahweh, and might be so actually if he realised his mission.

That our interpretation of ch. xlix. 1-6 is right, is clear from the verses that follow. Israel had been the servant of rulers (7), but now as Yahweh's servant was to summon the prisoners out of darkness. These are to come, it is said, not from Babylon, but from many distant lands: "Lo, these shall come from far: and, lo, these from the north and from the west: and these from the land of Sinim" (12). The return from Babylon was typical of a far larger and wider deliverance.

The leading idea of ch. xlii. is further developed in chs. lii. 13-liii. The chief thought of this passage is the contrast between future glory and past calamity. Captive Israel had been mocked by his enemies, maligned and ill-treated, "despised and rejected of men"; a poor, hopeless outcast, like a root in a barren soil, having no happiness to look forward to for himself or his offspring. And yet he had borne all this with dignity and patience. And now all was to be reversed. He would prosper, and be exalted very high. He would command the respect of the nations who had despised him. A victorious conqueror, he would divide his spoil with the strong. He would have a long and successful career, and finally would bequeath his prosperity to his descendants. He would "see his seed"; he would "prolong his days; the pleasure of Yahweh would prosper in his hand." We are reminded of those visions of national happiness which the prophets so frequently connected with the Restoration.

But this is only a broad outline of the passage. We have purposely reserved for more careful consideration, what is perhaps its most essential feature, and the special subject of our present discussion, the vicarious character of the sufferings of the Servant. It will be remembered that in the first message to captive Israel it was said, "She hath received of Yahweh's hand double for all her sins," *i.e.*, She had been punished twice as much as her sins deserved (Isa. xl. 2). It was but a step farther to regard Israel's sufferings as an atonement for the sins of other nations. God had punished Israel not so much for Israel's sake as for theirs. Through him they would be brought at last to perceive the arm of God (lii. 10, cf. liii. 1), which had been so long hidden by their own blindness; and would be able to say of Israel, "He was wounded for our transgressions, he was bruised for our iniquities: the chastisement of our peace was upon him; and with his stripes we are healed."[1] The nobility of suffering, the potency of sacrifice for a righteous cause —these were the great lessons which the Captivity had to teach, and such thoughts find expression in many a later psalm. It is of no little importance that

---

[1] Cf. Ibn Ezra's comment on the passage in *Rabbinical interpretations of Isa. liii.*—Neubauer and Driver.

L

parallel with these feelings there was the beginning of a new development in the doctrine of sacrifice which eventually found its most significant expression in the rites which marked the Great Day of Atonement.

There is one psalm which is connected by such sacred associations with the suffering Messiah of the Gospels that I cannot altogether pass it over. I refer to the twenty-second. It forms in some respects a parallel to Isa. lii. 13–liii. There is the same innocent suffering, the same scorn and persecution on the enemies' part, the same joyous termination, only in this case the end is still more glorious, at any rate, more evidently religious and spiritual. The sufferer released from his distress is to preach God's name till he converts all the nations of the world. Nor is the resemblance between the two really affected by the fact that the psalm is cast in a different mould; that here it is the sufferer himself who speaks of his persecutions, his prayer, and his final glorious mission. In this case again, it is obvious that the same question arises as before. Who is the subject of the psalm? Is it Christ Himself directly foretelling His Passion and work of salvation in the Christian Church? Or is it some Jewish martyr, Jeremiah for example, describing his own persecution and hopes? Or is it again some ideal personification of the whole or part of the Jewish nation?

1. The first alternative will not bear a thorough examination. For is it not obvious that the Psalmist is describing not a single occasion of accentuated

misery, but a long period of continued persecution; and, what is still more important, of incessant but fruitless prayer. Christ could not have said, "O my God, I cry in the daytime, but Thou answerest not; and in the night season, and am not silent" (2). To refer it to the agony on the Cross by day, the agony in the Garden of Gethsemane by night, shews a want of poetic feeling which amounts to serious ignorance. It is indeed somewhat difficult to separate the facts implied in the description from the metaphorical dress in which they are clothed. But what is certainly suggested is a general loss of bodily strength through different forms of privation, especially the loss of clothes, which his enemies take for themselves, like the rich oppressors so often condemned by the prophets;[1] and of food, so that the body is reduced to a living skeleton: "They may count all my bones" (14-18). It is obvious that these words are intended to portray an element in the sufferer's wretched condition. They cannot be meant to describe primarily the accidental honour paid by the Roman officials to our Lord's body in not breaking His legs.

It is not easy to decide between the two remaining alternatives of interpretation. For giving the psalm (2) a personal character there is much to be said. (*a*) To begin with, there is the negative reason that we have not here, as in Isa. liii., the strong argument from the whole surroundings of the passage, which almost compelled us to give a national sense to the

[1] See *e.g.* Amos ii. 6-8.

expression "Servant of Yahweh." A psalm will not from its very nature admit of an argument of that kind. (b) But, what is more important, the psalm itself gives at first sight the impression that we have here some Jewish martyr pouring out his own personal experience. Without is the bitter persecution to the death by a relentless and godless enemy. Within, the death-struggle and final triumph of a faith which determines, in spite of all difficulties, to believe in God's power and love. Had the psalm ended with the 21st verse, probably few would have any hesitation in accepting this view. But the last part of the psalm makes it very difficult to do so. It is not merely that the one oppressed martyr confidently asserts that he is to be the means of converting the whole world. This is startling enough [1]; but it is by no means an insuperable difficulty, if we believe that he is a type of the world's Great Martyr. The chief difficulty is that the subject of the preaching, the ground for conversion, is the goodness of God shewn in the deliverance of the Sufferer. We cannot understand the Psalmist conceiving such a thought of himself, nor would it be suitable if referred to the work of Christ. The subject of the gospel is not the deliverance of Christ, but the deliverance of man through Christ.

But these difficulties at once disappear if (3) we regard the Psalmist as personating the Jewish nation. The Jews, once scorned, impoverished, persecuted to the death by their godless enemies, were to become

[1] See Cheyne, *in loco*.

the missionaries of the whole world. All nations and all estates of men would worship Israel's God, Yahweh, and He would reign over the world from generation to generation. Thus understood, the last portion of the psalm is in thorough keeping with the familiar utterances of Messianic prophecy. No motive for the conversion of the nations is more frequent than the power of God manifested in the deliverance of His people from oppression. It may be possible, of course, that some later reviser added the last portion to the psalm, and so gave what was originally a personal psalm a national character. There are strong reasons for supposing that many of the psalms were thus revised and adapted for liturgical use.[1] But, on the other side, it may be reasonably argued that even in the first part (vv. 3-5) the Psalmist's grounds for trusting in God are not his own personal experiences of His goodness, but the favour shewn to the nation.

Let me now sum up the conclusion to which our inquiry seems to point. Suffering was not merely the punishment for sin, nor merely the vindication of God's righteousness, but the manifestation of His love, first for the good of the sufferer himself, and then through him of others. Hence came the thought, based on the fact of Israel's suffering, of an ideal suffering potent enough to heal the spiritual wounds, and bring about the salvation of all mankind. This was to be the work of Israel, himself purified and glorified through suffering. These thoughts were closely connected with the great Messianic hopes of the nation

[1] *E.g.* Pss. li. lxxvii.

which were raised by the prophets, but they were not so closely, if at all, connected with the personal Messiah. Yet they were the moral force which produced what was noblest and best in the Jewish character, which evoked the spirit of patriotic religious zeal, that inspired the great Maccabæan martyrs; and though it at times blazed forth in acts of religious fanaticism, has often enabled the Jews to bear unspeakable wrongs with a wonderful patience and hope.

In saying this we do not forget the most perfect example of this spirit, One Who raised it to an infinitely higher level than it had hitherto attained, the depths of Whose soul were stirred with sadness for the fate of His people, in spite of all the wrong which He was suffering at their hands; Who on the cross bare the sin of many, and made intercession for the transgressors; Who through His sufferings won a great crown of glory, not for Himself alone, but for the whole of humanity. But while we remember all this, we must not limit these truths of Hebrew prophecy to Jesus of Nazareth. They are principles in the moral world of God, of which Jesus was indeed the one perfect example; but they are exemplified in a measure also in all those who, following their Great Captain, suffer in the cause of righteousness and truth, and so, to use the impressive language of St Paul, "fill up that which is lacking of the afflictions of Christ for His body's sake, which is the Church."[1] "If we died with Him, we shall also live with Him; if we endure, we shall also reign with Him."[2]

[1] Col. i. 24.   [2] 2 Tim. ii. 11, 12.

CHAPTER X

THE FULFILMENT OF PROPHECY IN CHRISTIANITY

"All things therefore whatsoever ye would that men should do unto you, even so do ye also unto them: for this is the law and the prophets."—MATT. vii. 12.

THE argument from prophecy may be said to involve three questions—(1) What did the prophets predict? (2) How and to what extent were their predictions fulfilled? (3) What bearing has their fulfilment on the evidences for the truth of Christianity? The first of these questions would, at first sight, seem very simple. And it may be thought that an undue proportion of this book has been occupied in discussing it. But we have constantly found it necessary to reckon with an old system of interpretation which more scholarly methods of study have shewn to be misleading. We have now to consider the second question.

But first let me summarise briefly the results of our former inquiry. A populous nation of Jews and Israelites united in one body politic, in a prodigiously fertile country, living in godliness and righteousness, with all that constitutes outward prosperity, under a perfect King, who is the head of a world-wide empire, in the centre of a world-wide Church. Such is the rough outline of the picture of the golden age which we have found drawn for us by the prophets. Each prophet, it is true, dwells with a special emphasis on one or another of the different parts of the picture; each fills up the outline in his own way, and throws something of his own character and feeling into his drawing. But there is no part of the picture which does not, in one form or another, occur frequently in the prophetic pages. Now, did the event justify the prophets' expectation? If we take the whole picture as I have described it, we are bound in honesty to answer "No." There may have been periods of great agricultural prosperity. There certainly were times, as in the Maccabæan wars, when the prowess and the success of the Jews in battle seems all but miraculous. But these, great as they were, were very much less than what the prophets' language must have led men to hope. From a purely political point of view, it must be confessed that the Maccabæan struggles ended in failure. The final resort to Roman protection was the death-blow to that national greatness which the prophets loved to depict. As for the perfect king who was to bring all nations into subjection to Judæa, where are we to look for him in Jewish history? The nearest approach is to be found in the priest-princes of the Asmonean line; but even the most successful of these, Hyrcanus, hardly extended the subject territory beyond the limits of Solomon's empire. Still less can we look for the prophets' Messiah in the Herods. What would the Prophet of the Captivity or Malachi have felt, could they have risen from the dead, to behold an Edomite reigning as king of Judæa? (See Isa. lxiii. 1-6; Mal. i. 2-5.)

Have we any right, then, to say that these prophecies have been fulfilled? This is the question which the apologist must candidly answer. It will be perfectly useless to contend that something else was fulfilled which sceptics will never be got to believe that the prophets predicted at all. I think we must begin by candidly and unreservedly admitting that the prophets were mistaken in all of what we may call the outward aspects of their Messianic hope. We do not, of course, include under this heading the purely imaginative settings of some of their prophecies. But leaving them out of the question, we have no reason to think that *they* made any distinction between what was external and what was internal. In all probability they believed in the fulfilment of the one quite as much as of the other. But, on the other hand, we acknowledge that, taking the prophets as a whole, the inward and spiritual side is dwelt upon with greater earnestness, and as of far greater importance. Looking back, *we* at any rate can separate the outward and the spiritual; and while we admit, without hesitation, that the first has not been fulfilled, we can say that that does not of itself preclude the claim for the fulfilment of the second.

But before we proceed to consider this claim, there is a further point which cannot be overlooked. It may be urged that although these, so to speak, temporal and political prophecies were not literally fulfilled, they were fulfilled spiritually. That is to say, that the outward aspects of the prophecies were types or figures bearing some analogy to Christian antitypes. Now it cannot be reasonably denied, to take a striking example of this method of spiritual interpretation, that it is a great help to us Christians in giving shape to our religious conceptions, to think of the Church as a kingdom under the government of our Priest-King; and we have the authority of Christ Himself for the use of such metaphors, but not for pressing them too far.[1] And the same, no doubt, may be said, more or less, of many other spiritual or, as they are sometimes called, analogical interpretations. But that is not the real question at issue. What we have to ask is not whether certain ideas are beautiful or helpful in themselves, but whether, regarded as fulfilments of prophecies, they have any evidential value. If they have any, it must be very small compared with that of an argument derived from the direct fulfilment of prophetic expectation. For example, we may perhaps feel justified in explaining the reference of the words, "I called My son out of Egypt" (Hos. xi. 1) to Christ, by the theory that Christ in a sense represents the whole spiritual Israel, of which the literal Israel was a type; but it

---

[1] It is curious to notice how very few of the parables of the kingdom bear out the analogy which their title would lead us to expect. A conquering king, the chief element of the prophets' Messianic kingdom is conspicuously absent. The very idea of an external kingdom is, perhaps, positively contradicted in Luke xvii. 21.

would be quite unjustifiable to quote these words of Hosea as a proof that the prophet was possessed of supernatural foresight. Supposing again that a sceptic were to say this, "Isaiah plainly foretold a great earthly king, to say the least, far surpassing all the kings that were before him in earthly power and moral goodness, but such a king never came,"—what should our answer be? Should we say, "Yes, Isaiah's prophecies were fulfilled; the king came, but He was a Spiritual King, ruling over the hearts of men"? To us that is true enough. But can we imagine the sceptic being the least convinced. He would certainly say, "I do not for one moment believe that Isaiah meant anything of the kind." What we want are not defences to cover our retreat, but weapons to carry into the enemies' camp, or rather, should I not say, that power of enforcing belief which can only come out of a thorough and honest conviction of our own.

Now, as distinct from this so-called spiritual fulfilment of temporal prophecies, what do we mean by the inward and spiritual predictions of the prophets? Let us avoid at all cost mere vague generalities. We mean, then, that the Jewish prophets were the pioneers in religion. While they shewed sin in its true light, they put forth a standard of moral goodness and religious purity far before their time. Their religious prophecies, in the narrower sense of the word, were in close connexion with their whole attitude towards religion. They moulded a religion which for spirituality and depth has surpassed every other which the world has ever known, except one other, if indeed it can be called another. It is difficult in a moment to appreciate the full force of this fact. For (1) an uncritical study of the Old Testament has, by antedating so much of the religious ideas of the nation, tended to obscure the spiritual work of the prophets. It must make a very great difference in our estimate of their work, if we have once realised that the Book of Deuteronomy is the impulse of a great religious awakening, parallel with that outburst of prophecy, which marked the golden age of Jewish literature. (2) What is more important still, the lofty spiritual teaching of the prophets and psalmists has by long habit of thought become completely blended with the Christian teaching of the New Testament. And so it is extremely difficult for us to realise, if I may so put it, how much Christianity there was before the time of Christ. But it is of the utmost importance to grasp this fact, if we are to do justice to the great saints of the Old Testament. Though the light was shining in darkness, it was even then lightening every one according as he had the power of receiving it. Christian apologists, naturally enough, make a great deal of the fact that there was among the Jews an expectation of a personal Messiah. But after all it is of infinitely greater importance to bear in mind that the seeds of a deeply spiritual religion, sown by the prophets and watered by the psalmists, had been growing in the hearts of the more pious Jews; and that when Christ came it could be said of some, even of those who though outside the pale of Judaism were not altogether outside its deeper influences, that they were " white already unto harvest" (John iv. 35). The growth of the Λόγος doctrine has a theological interest which I do not wish for a moment to underrate ; but how much more important would it be for the history of religious thought and feeling if we could enter fully into the mind and character of a Simeon or an Anna.

It would be an almost impossible task to attempt to shew in detail how the Old Testament saints anticipate the teaching of Christ and His apostles. All that I can attempt to do is to mention a few great leading thoughts which will be sufficient to explain my meaning, and possibly serve as an outline for others to fill in for themselves. (1) The first thing that strikes us is the lofty conception of God Himself. It would hardly be an exaggeration to say that of such splendid thoughts as find expression in Faber's hymn " My God, how wonderful Thou art," there is not one to which we could not find a parallel in the Old Testament. The spiritual nature of God is nowhere perhaps more forcibly expressed than in Ps. cxxxix., its moral beauty than in Isa. lv. We may, indeed, reasonably believe that the spirit of the psalm is more real to us than it could have been to those who first knew it. But that is just because Christianity has so frequently enforced the truth which the psalmists felt as, so to speak, a personal inspiration.

On the other hand, some thoughts of God, His absolute greatness, His "awful purity" appear to have been even more keenly felt by some of the inspired Jews than by certainly the great bulk of Christian saints. For is it not a patent fact, however much we may rightly deplore it, that our familiarity—I know no other word to express my meaning—our familiarity with Christ has tended to obscure the absolute greatness of God? And yet the latter is obviously in accord with the best teaching of Christianity. The fault then is clearly not due to any failure of Christianity to reach the lofty religious ideal of the prophets and psalmists in this respect, but to the failure of many Christians to maintain the full teaching of Christianity itself. (2) To take another point, the soul's sense of the need of spiritual communion with God. Where in Christian literature is this more forcibly expressed than in Ps. lxiii. 1-4: "O God, Thou art my God; early will I seek Thee: my soul thirsteth for Thee, my flesh longeth for Thee, in a dry and weary land, where no water is"? Or again in Ps. xlii. 1, 2: "As the hart panteth after the water brooks, so panteth my soul after Thee, O God. My soul thirsteth for God, for the living God: when shall I come and appear before God?" (3) Take again the sense of sin as a separation from God. Where can we find this more deeply felt than in Ps. li.? Or (4) again, the converse of this, purity of life as an essential condition of communion with God? With what an eloquent simplicity is this truth enforced in

Ps. xxiv. 3-5 : " Who shall ascend into the hill of Yahweh? and who shall stand in His holy place? He that hath clean hands, and a pure heart; who hath not lifted up his soul unto vanity, and hath not sworn deceitfully. He shall receive a blessing from Yahweh, and righteousness from the God of his salvation." It is a remarkable fact how in every age of Christianity, men have found in the Psalms the most perfect expression of religious devotion.

And yet this intrinsically religious character of the Psalms may be turned into an objection to our argument. It may be said that such expressions as I have quoted describe the existing religious feelings of the several writers at the time when they wrote; they are not, and do not profess to be, prophecies of a religion to come. This is true, no doubt. Though we might have quoted many somewhat similar passages from the prophets, especially from Isaiah, we certainly do find the deeper expression of religious feeling more frequently in the Psalms. But the objection misses the point. What is here contended for is that the prophets were, humanly speaking, the source and mainspring of such religious feelings. At a time when religion in its best and truest sense was all but dead, and common morality was hardly known, the prophets put before men ideals of personal religion as things both possible and worth aiming after. More than this, every now and then, in flights of religious hope, they confidently asserted that the time would come when these ideals would be realised. Look, for example, at Jer. xxxi. 33, 34: "This is the covenant that I will make with the house of Israel after those days, saith Yahweh: I will put My law in their inward parts, and in their heart will I write it; and I will be their God, and they shall be My people." Look again at Ezek. xi. 19, 20: "I will give them one (LXX. more probably "another") heart, and I will put a new spirit within you; and I will take the stony heart out of their flesh, and will give them an heart of flesh: that they may walk in My statutes, and keep Mine ordinances, and do them."

But a more serious objection to our argument is that it proves too much. If the Psalms are as a whole, as critics say, later than the Prophets, it may be argued that we have in the Psalms already the fulfilment of the spiritual prophecies. We have no need, therefore, to look for it to Christianity. This is, no doubt, so far true that we must admit a certain degree of fulfilment in the spiritual religion to which the Psalms testify. But can it be seriously denied that there was a more perfect fulfilment in the teaching of Christ? For (1) in the Psalms we find expressions such as the deprecations of enemies, which fall far below the Christian standard. In some cases it may be that the Psalms in which they occur belong to preprophetic Judaism, but in many it is extremely improbable. For example, the phrase, "Let the praises of God be in their mouth, and a two-edged sword in their hand" (Ps. xlix. 6), is specially suited to the fierce religious patriotism of the Maccabæan era. (2) Again, absolute unselfishness is a duty which finds no place in the Psalter, and yet it was with respect to this doctrine of all others that Christ claimed that His teaching was a fulfilment of prophetic Judaism: "All things whatsoever ye would that men should do unto you, even so do ye also unto them: for this is the law and the prophets." The so-called law of Moses, and still more the prophets, by insisting on a kindly feeling towards the poor and the oppressed, paved the way for the more perfect teaching of Christ. We can thus fairly say that the prophets set forth a religious standard which was not perfected until Christ came.

And when we pass from the moral and devotional side of Christianity to its more distinctive theology, we find the same thing. Hosea had indeed taught the fatherly love of God, but chiefly with reference to the nation as a whole; with Christ the consciousness of it first becomes an abiding influence in the religious life of the individual. So, too, with the Incarnation. It would be an anachronism to say that the prophets predict an incarnate God, but they did certainly lead men in the way of feeling after it. We see indications of this, no doubt, in the kingly, the priestly and, perhaps we should add, the prophetic Messiah of the prophets, which shew a tendency to connect the highest hope of the Jews with a unique Personality. But we see them more evidently in those prophecies which shew the yearning and the promise of the presence of God among men. For

M

what the prophets have to tell us is not so much the form which Christianity was to take, as its renovating power.

And so again with the Atonement. It may not be true that the prophets and psalmists contemplated a suffering Messiah, as I pointed out in the last chapter, but at any rate they set forth an ideal of innocent suffering as a power in the regeneration of man. This ideal is undoubtedly connected with the Jewish nation in Isa. liii., and probably also in Ps. xxii. But the personification in both cases made it easier to see that the suffering Christ was a unique fulfilment of the ideal: "He was despised and rejected of men; a man of sorrows, and acquainted with grief: and as one from whom men hide their face He was despised, and we esteemed Him not. Surely He hath borne our griefs, and carried our sorrows. . . . He was wounded for our transgressions, He was bruised for our iniquities; the chastisement of our peace was upon Him; and with His stripes we are healed." How can Christians help seeing in such language words infinitely truer of Jesus Christ than of any other person?

And the same is also true of the doctrine of the Holy Spirit. It may be extremely difficult to say what was the precise meaning which prophet or psalmist attached to the phrases, "the Spirit of God" and "the Spirit of holiness." But such language at any rate shews that they realised the divine character of that inward power which makes for holiness and truth. "Cast me not away from Thy presence, and take not the Spirit of Thy holiness from me" (Ps. li. 11). "And now the Lord God hath sent me, and His Spirit" (Isa. xlviii. 16). "Not by might, nor by power, but by My Spirit, saith Yahweh of hosts" (Zech. iv, 6). In such passages as these, we can see the germ of the fuller Christian thought.

But what of the other distinctive doctrines of Christianity, and especially those of the resurrection from the dead and life everlasting? We surely cannot, in the light of modern scholarship, say confidently that the writers of the Old Testament predicted these. But if they did not predict them, they were, as it were, feeling after them. We may have great uncertainty about the meaning of Ezek. xxxvii. or Isa. xxvi. The resurrection of Israel may in either case be, and in Ezekiel probably is, nothing more than a poetical figure. We may have grave doubts about the nature of Job's great hope.[1] But when we come to the Psalms, we begin to find expressions, which are most naturally explained of some kind of belief in a future state: "I shall be satisfied, when I awake, with Thy likeness;" "The upright shall have dominion over them in the morning;" and, above all, that marvellous flight of religious hope, "Thou wilt not leave my soul to Sheol; neither wilt thou suffer Thine holy one (or holy ones) to see the pit. Thou wilt shew me the path of life: in Thy presence is fulness of joy; in Thy right hand there are pleasures for

[1] Job xix. 25-27.

evermore."[1] In the time of the Maccabees we find what had been the exceptional effort of faith becoming the settled conviction of, at least, the most pious Jews. Probably it was the persecutions of those troublous times which especially tended to strengthen it. And the distinct belief in this doctrine at that time helps to explain the language of the Psalms. The growth of religious thought among a people is like the growth of speech in a child. There is a time in his life when his cries are quite inarticulate. A little later, and there are sounds which to the mother's ear alone seem like the first efforts after certain words. A little later still, and a few intelligible words can be clearly distinguished, which prove that the mother was right. Just in the same way the more developed thought of later Judaism shews us that in phrases which seem at first sight vague and ambiguous, the Psalmists were endeavouring to give expression to a half-conscious hope that communion with God would not be altogether cut asunder by death.

We see a still more striking example of the true relation between prophecy and fulfilment in what bears upon the rejection of the Jews and the admission of the Gentiles. That many of the prophets contemplated the admission of the Gentiles into the Jewish Church is abundantly evident. But it is also true that it was almost always connected with some sort of subordination of the Gentiles to Israel. No prophet, for example, more clearly recognised that all nations were under

[1] Ps. xvii. 15; xlix. 14; xvi. 10, 11.

God's sovereignty than Amos. And yet, when Israel has been sifted by punishment, this prophet expressly promises the possession of Edom, and of all the nations which are called by God's name (Amos ix. 12). We cannot, then, suppose that the prophets seriously contemplated the rejection of God's people in favour of the Gentiles. But there is no real difficulty in this, if we believe that the outward aspects of the prophecy were dictated by the same patriotic spirit which loved to picture a Jewish king ruling over a Jewish world. The germ of such prophecies lies in the feeling after the thought that the one religion of the future was to break down all distinctions of race. It is the spirit in which St Paul uttered the noble hyperbole: "There can be neither Jew nor Greek, there can be neither bond nor free, there can be no male and female: for ye are all one [man] in Christ Jesus" (Gal. iii. 28). And besides, is it quite correct to speak of the rejection of the Jews? To those Jews who rejected Christ, was not their severance their own act of faithlessness to their own creed? We may say, "But does not St Paul speak of the Jewish apostasy as part of a providential dispensation?" Yes, but we must also remember that to St Paul the final salvation of the Jews was an essential corollary of his argument. It is not fair to accept the one and to ignore the other.

To sum up briefly what I have said, we may say that prophecy is fulfilled in Christianity in the following ways :—(1) Christianity enforced the high religious and moral standards of the prophets. (2) It confirmed the religious truths which the prophets taught. (3) It gave to both a more perfect and complete development. (4) Christ brought into the world a new potent force, and so the fulfilment of the prophets' ideals of life and conduct was made more and more possible, a fulfilment which the prophets had foretold as a glorious hope. (5) In Christ the religion of a nation became, as the prophets have foretold, potentially at least, the religion of the world.

These facts are in principle coming to be recognised more and more by Jewish writers themselves. Read, *e.g.*, what Graetz says in his *History of the Jews*:[1] "The time had come," he writes, speaking of the Christian era, "when the fundamental truths of Judaism, till then only thoroughly known and rightly appreciated by profound thinkers, should burst their shackles, and go freely forth among all the people of the earth. Sublime and lofty views of God and of holy living for the individual as well as for the state, which form the kernel of Judaism, were now to permeate among other nations, and to bring them a rich and beneficent harvest. Israel was now to commence in earnest her sacred mission; she was to become the teacher of nations. The ancient teaching about God and religious morality was to be introduced by her into a godless and immoral world. Judaism, however, could only gain admission into the hearts of the heathens by taking another name and assuming new forms." If Jews are willing to admit such a strong

[1] Eng. Trans. vol. ii. p. 141.

argument as this for Christianity, Christians need not shrink from admitting what Christ Himself insisted on: "Think not that I came to destroy the law or the prophets: I came not to destroy, but to fulfil" (Matt. v. 17). It was not of any real or fancied foreshadowings of His person or His work that Christ uttered these words, but of the eternal, but gradually revealed, truths of religion and morality.

CHAPTER XI

PROGRESSIVE CHRISTIANITY THE MOST PERFECT FULFILMENT OF JEWISH PROPHECY

"Think not that I came to destroy the law, or the prophets: I came not to destroy, but to fulfil."—MATT. v. 17.

I ENDEAVOURED to shew in the last chapter that the truest fulfilment of prophecy lies not so much in the personality and work of Christ as in the religion of Christ. But what is the precise meaning of this last phrase? Is it primitive Christianity, or the Christianity of the early centuries, or mediæval Christianity, or the Christianity of the Reformed Churches, or the Christianity of the nineteenth century as we find it in England? Or is it none of these as such, but rather Christianity as taught by Christ and His apostles? For surely we cannot, without some confusion of thought, regard all these as absolutely identical.

As regards the first, we are indeed apt to assume, on *a priori* grounds, a purity in the early Church of which we have little or no evidence. Indeed the evidence seems rather to prove the opposite. The First Epistle to the Corinthians points to a state of life and religion, the very thought of which is repulsive to the average Christian of to-day. We read of disorders taking place in the church services of Corinth which would now be thought disgraceful at a meeting of a School Board or of a Parish Council; of the Holy Communion being converted into something too like a drunken brawl; of an incestuous alliance uncondemned by public opinion. In a word, not only could primitive Christianity fail in practice, but its standards, as commonly accepted, might be very low. It may be urged that in all probability the Church of Corinth was an exception to the general rule; that we do not hear of such things in other Churches; at any rate, that that particular Church was subject to many special difficulties and temptations. This may have been the case, to some extent; but, on the other hand, it must be borne in mind that it is the only Church of which we really know much. There are also in the other Epistles too many hints of dark sinister influences which were tainting the religious and social life.[1] Nor can we urge, on the other side, the lofty standard of St. Paul's own teaching; for that was plainly the ideal which Christians should aim at rather than a description of what they actually were.

As we proceed further in the history of the Church, we see the effects of the chastening power of persecution in producing a character heroic and loyal, but for all that somewhat stern and narrow. At the same time we begin to trace, mainly through the influence of the schools of Alexandria and Antioch, a new

[1] *E.g.* 1 Thess. iv. 5, 6; Phil. iii. 2; Rev. ii. 14.

principle of intellectual life infusing itself into the simple and somewhat crude faith of the early Church, and making Christianity more capable of becoming the religion of the cultured classes. There is something obviously incomplete in the ante-Nicene Church. It belongs to an age of growth and preparation. Taken by itself, we cannot regard it as the fulfilment of an ideal.

With the conversion of Constantine, we reach a new stage in the history of Christianity. On the one hand, we see the Christian Church reaping all the benefits of Roman civilisation. It is an age of organisation. Liturgies, creeds, church offices are systematised and arranged, or their arrangement already begun is now completed. On the other hand, we see the entrance of a secular and ambitious spirit taking the place of the austere unselfishness of the early Christian. And again, as a counterpoise to this, we trace from this time the rapid development of monasticism. Men and women, vexed with the theological controversies of the age or disgusted with its secularity, sought to find in seclusion that religious whole-heartedness which they had failed to find in the world or even in the Church. That the monasteries did a great work in the history of Christianity, that their inmates aimed at living a nobly Christian life, cannot seriously be denied. It was they who kept religion safely stored as in a sacred shrine when it was in danger of being overwhelmed by the flood of semibarbarism that swept over Western Europe. But a religion, in its deeper spiritual life almost confined to those who abjured a sinful world, was a very different thing from the world-wide Church foretold by the prophets and Christ. The monastic system was in fact a confession of failure to realise in life the Christian ideal.

And what are we to say of the Papal Church of the Middle Ages? Shall we allow the bitterness of party strife to blind our judgment? Shall we ignore its historical connexion with the Christianity that preceded it? Shall we overlook its real work in Christian history? Shall we see in it nothing better than a fulfilment of those prophecies of the New Testament which speak of a great corrupting power hostile to God and to His Church, to be eventually overthrown and cursed amid the exultations of her enemy? To do so would be as unjust as it would be ungenerous. For is it not obvious, if we study those prophecies which in the bitterness of controversy have been unscrupulously hurled at Papal Rome, that many of them are directed against an avowed and open enemy to the Christian Church? Nor is it altogether surprising that the son of thunder, himself the victim of a cruel persecution, in thus gathering up and applying to imperial Rome the threats of the earlier Jewish prophets against their several foes,—a Tyre, an Assyria, or a Babylon,—should have shewn something of the vindictive spirit of the old religion. We may be thankful, indeed, that in this case, as in the story of Jonah, God was in the event more merciful than His prophet. Rome was not permitted to fall into the hands of its barbarian conquerors until what in it was most worth preserving had become the possession of Christianity, and out of the ruins of the old civil Rome rose a new spiritual empire, the great hierarchy of Western Christendom. In spite of its narrow ecclesiasticism, in spite of its spiritual arrogance, the papacy of Hildebrand was a magnificent attempt to realise the prophecies of the kingdom of God upon earth. No wonder that men, dazzled by its splendour, should have so often been blind to its shortcomings. But the papacy failed just because it made the same mistake which Jewish patriotism had made before. It could not distinguish between a spiritual theocracy and an earthly dominion.

And what of the Reformed Churches? I suppose we may say that the leading principle of the Reformation was that each nation should form a separate ecclesiastical unit, developing itself in various directions according to its special needs, while still united to the Church as a whole on certain cardinal points of doctrine and practice.[1] But there were numerous difficulties in carrying out this principle. (1) Certain nations, even in Western Europe, to say nothing of the Eastern Church, refused to accept it altogether, and adhered to the old hierarchical idea of Catholicity. (2) Among those nations which accepted the principle, there was a serious disagreement as to what should be retained as essential elements of Catholicity. For instance, the Lutheran Church,

[1] In England, at any rate, this principle was not altogether new.

with possibly one exception,[1] repudiated the apostolic succession of bishops. The English Church, in spite of what Roman controversialists have often said to the contrary, made a point of retaining it. Again, on such an important subject as the efficacy of the sacraments, there were the most important differences, not of degree only, but of kind. Lutherans, Calvinists, Zwinglians were on this point as far removed from each other as the Lutherans were from the Church of Rome, and the upshot of it all was, that many of the Reformed Churches practically gave up all idea of Catholic Unity. (3) A far more serious difficulty lay in the refusal of many within the reformed nationalities, if I may use the expression, to accept the principle of a national Church established by authority. The process of disintegration did not stop at the point which the civil authorities desired. Innumerable sects sprang up everywhere within the several nations, and neither king nor Parliament found it in the end either possible or desirable to check them. For they lacked those religious weapons which had bound kings and people under the yoke of the papacy. How, then, can we see in this divided Church of modern Christendom, or in any one division of it, or in any one body of Christians, a fulfilment of Christ's prophecies of the kingdom of God?

And when we pass from questions of belief and organisation to those of life and character, the difficulty

[1] Some English writers have affirmed that the apostolic succession was maintained in Sweden.

of doing so becomes even greater. What are we to think about war, for example? If there is one distinct promise of Jewish prophecy, it is that of universal peace. We cannot surely class the prophecies which speak of it with those which foretell the universal dominion of the Jews, and call them utopian dreams, the offspring of a one-sided patriotism. It is true, no doubt, that a certain number were coloured by thoughts of this kind. But there is enough to shew that the peace of the world-wide Church was expected as an inseparable outshoot from religious character. " And many nations shall go, and say, Come ye, and let us go up to the mountain of Yahweh, and to the house of the God of Jacob; and He will teach us of His ways, and we will walk in His paths: for out of Zion shall go forth the law, and the word of Yahweh from Jerusalem. And He shall judge between many peoples, and shall reprove strong nations afar off; and they shall beat their swords into plowshares, and their spears into pruning hooks: nation shall not lift up sword against nation, neither shall they learn war any more. . . . For all the peoples will walk every one in the name of his god, and we will walk in the name of Yahweh our God for ever and ever" (Mic. iv. 2-5). So, too, in Isaiah's prophecy of the holy mountain (ch. xi. 1-9) the point of the parabolic picture is that the character of the wild animals is so changed that they no longer have any wish to destroy and devour each other. But what do we see now? We see the most civilised nations of Europe year by year increasing their armaments, nation vying with nation, party with party; we find the question how, when and where the next great European war will break out, debated in our daily newspapers with the calmness that we should expect in a leader on the prospects of the next general election. It seems as though the "herald angels" must sometimes weep to see Christians so dazzled by the outward glories of war as to forget its countless horrors and miseries.

Then, again, in any Christian nation, what comparison do the ordinary standards of life bear to those of Christianity as Christ taught it? In those countless falsities—*e.g.* those many conventional tricks of trade, those only too common professional and social lies, even in those petty hypocrisies of the drawing-room—there is a want of Christian manliness which makes some men sigh for the departed spirit of sturdy English Puritanism. Take again the great social question. Is it not truly piteous that in Christian England a very large and increasing section of our countrymen should be living lives of physical and moral misery, cut off from almost everything that gives life pleasure; and, worse still, that so large a number of Christian gentlemen and gentlewomen should practically acquiesce in such a state of things? Christian England has yet to learn that to raise the condition of the poor,—I do not say to support them, —is an infinitely more important duty than joining in family prayer or hearing a weekly sermon. Need

I point out, also, how very far in purity of life we fall short of the standard of Christ and His apostles?

We are bound, then, sadly to confess that no single period of Church history, no one division of those who call themselves Christians, has yet realised the ideal of Christianity. But it is this ideal which stands in direct relation to Jewish prophecy. It is of it that Christ said: "I came not to destroy but to fulfil." But is not to say this to reduce to a vanishing point the argument from prophecy? Is it not equivalent to saying that Christ Himself is but a Prophet, and that Christianity is all the more utopian than the earlier prophecies, in so far as its ideals are loftier, and for that very reason impose a greater strain on human nature? How can these earlier prophecies claim a fulfilment in a number of religious and social theories which have never been worked out consistently and thoroughly into a practical living system?

But to say this is to exaggerate the true state of the case. For there is hardly a single element of the religious and spiritual side of Jewish prophecy which has not been *partially* fulfilled in Christian history. The great Christian doctrines of the Fatherhood of God, the presence of Christ through sacramental grace, the influence of the Holy Spirit, were, as we have already pointed out, fulfilments of the prophet's teaching. But they are not merely so many theological propositions; they have exercised a force which has been more and more making itself felt, and leavening society. There has been growing through the ages a kindlier spirit between nation and nation, class and class, sex and sex. "There can be neither Jew nor Greek, there can be neither bond nor free, there can be no male and female: for ye all are one man in Christ Jesus" (Gal. iii. 28). With St Paul these words were a prophecy, with us they have in part at least become history. Slavery already stands in direct opposition to our ideas of modern civilisation. Women are less and less excluded from opportunities of culture and positions of healthy independence. Above all, every year sees fresh, and, in a measure, successful efforts to promote the welfare of those whom we are beginning to call no longer the lower classes. After all, the seeming apathy of the better-to-do arises, in a very great measure, from the difficulties which beset the social question. It is quite possible to feel a glow of enthusiasm for that noble effort of the primitive Church of Jerusalem to organise the social life in the loving spirit of their great Master, and yet feel bound to confess that even then the experiment proved a failure.

But if they did these things in the green tree, what has been done in the dry? What can we think of the modern substitutes for that first outburst of Christian Socialism?—An enforced poor-rate, a fraction of which only is spent on the poor, and that too often in a way which tends to pauperise and degrade them: a weekly church collection of petty sums, which mean the sacrifice of not a single luxury or pleasure on the part of those who give them: the distribution of promiscuous alms, that bane of charity organisations. How difficult it is, without doing positive harm, to bring our dealings with the poor into any sort of relation with the spirit of Christ? And how easy it is to allow the possible harm, or the probable harm, of misspent charity to harden us against what we know and feel to be a Christian duty? It is so easy to give our weekly sixpence or our weekly half-crown, and flatter ourselves that we are not tainted with the old socialistic heresy of the Anabaptists. But the spirit of the age is, after all, too honest to deceive itself by such a miserable compromise. Amid all its perplexity, it is, at any rate, feeling after Christianity.

And yet again there is a further difficulty. The great poor questions of the day are becoming so mixed up with the miserable contentions of party politics. There is an increasing tendency to make political capital out of a compulsion which may to many seem unjust, but to none can be inspiring. It may seem a thing too bold to say, and yet I suspect that it is true, that if our poor laws could be swept away entirely, and the relief of the poor left to voluntary effort, there would be, before very long, an immense improvement in their condition. The Church of England, and not the Church of England alone, but other religious bodies, would feel bound to throw themselves into the work of poor relief heart and soul. They would feel that it really was their work, and that they were not patching up what was already being done very inadequately by the State. The love of Christ would inspire energy and enthusiasm. They would take up the work in the same spirit as the early Church and the monasteries, but with the wisdom of a ripe experience. Is it not also true that the new opportunities for work and self-denial would strengthen Christian faith among us? Men would surely realise more and more, what is now too often half forgotten, that Christianity is not so much a thing to be learnt as a life to be lived.

We have aimed at shewing, by a few examples, that the Church of Christ has in the past already begun at least to fulfil in a measure the splendid prophecies of the Jewish prophets as confirmed and developed by Christ. But we may go a step further than this, and say that Christianity contains within itself forces which seem surely tending to a much more perfect fulfilment in the future. We see this tendency, e.g., in foreign missions. It cannot be denied that this work is steadily increasing in extent, in earnestness, and in power. It used to be a common thing among men of culture to speak contemptuously of missionary labours. To do so now would shew not only bad taste, but serious ignorance. A spiritual kingdom of the world is already to us something more than a religious theory; it is becoming a historical fact. Christianity already exercises an incomparably greater civilising force than any other religion.

We see the same tendency even in the Christian attitude towards war. If a world-wide peace seems as yet very far from coming into the sphere of practical politics, there is at least a perceptible movement in this direction. Men are beginning more and more to feel that war, though often perhaps at present necessary, is at best a necessary evil. The prospect of war with a Christian nation, at any rate, is becoming more and more repulsive. Again, wars are becoming far less sanguinary. Some of the worst evils of war are mitigated by the humanity and even tenderness shewn to the wounded. There is a tendency, though but a slowly increasing tendency, to settle international disputes by arbitration. It is also more than probable that the maintenance of a balance of power by means of defensive alliances has in itself, for many years, proved a safeguard against a European war.

Again, to speak of our social relations, it may be true that class barriers are still too artificial and classes too exclusive; but with the wider diffusion of culture and education this is becoming less and less the case. There is every probability that as differences between classes are obliterated, distinctions will gradually disappear also. As it is, men and women of different social grades are more and more inclined to work together in harmony for some common cause.

Above all, we see the same tendency in religious parties. Efforts are increasingly being made to bring together those separated by religious differences. Even though such efforts may not at present have succeeded to the extent, or in the exact way, that their promoters wished, they have at least shewn that there is a movement towards religious concord.

More than this, they have actually done much to promote mutual understanding and sympathy.

If, then, the prophets and Christian ideals have been, and are being, more and more perfectly fulfilled in Christian history, is it unreasonable to believe that the time will come when, in the highest and truest sense, the kingdoms of the world will become the kingdom of the Lord and of His Christ?

It is a common temptation to take a pessimistic view of the age in which we live. We may be inclined to sigh over its open infidelity, its selfish anarchy, its dissoluteness. But these are not the distinctive evils of our age exclusively. In part, they are always with us; in part, they have repeated themselves many times in human history. It is our duty to struggle against them and try to overcome them. But we can only hope to do so effectually if we listen to that voice of God which called almost in vain to the ancient Israelites through the prophets, and still calls to us through the Son of God: "All things whatsoever ye would that men should do unto you, even so do ye also unto them: for this is the law and the prophets."

CHAPTER XII

THE PRACTICAL VALUE OF PROPHECY AS AN AID TO CHRISTIAN FAITH

"Prove all things; hold fast that which is good."—1 THESS. v. 21.

IT will be my aim in this last chapter to put together in some practical form the evidential value of prophecy. Christian evidences are not at present a very attractive branch of theology. They are often associated with books which to us of the present day seem hard and dry, to lack life and humanity, to be out of touch with our own thought and experience. More serious than this, the argument from prophecy as frequently put forward in them is, in the light of modern criticism and scholarship, not only useless, but mischievous. I may, then, perhaps be pardoned if I even go so far in an opposite direction as to avoid altogether a formal argument, and endeavour to express in a different manner what I conceive to be the value of Jewish prophecy in promoting Christian faith. What is needed is not so much an academic formula, as a convincing proof of the power of prophecy to promote faith in God and Christ. And I think I shall be most likely to explain adequately what I believe this power may be, if, by taking a typical case, I can shew it, so to speak, at work in human life.

Let us then, by way of example, suppose a young man with an average general and religious education, who, after having for many years learnt what others have thought, has now begun definitely to think for himself, and finds himself for the first time face to face with the religious problem. He is startled to discover some sort of discrepancies between his religious ideas and his ordinary modes of thought. He searches himself, and takes count of himself to find out, not what he has been taught to believe, or ought to believe, or thinks that he believes, but what he does believe.

Now, such a person might very reasonably, I think, argue much in this way. " I find in myself a natural love of goodness. I feel a pleasure in the sense of doing good, whether in the present or prospectively, which I cannot satisfactorily compare with any other pleasure. The difference cannot be expressed to my mind by any words implying merely greater or less intensity. Other pleasures may, indeed, be far more intense. It is obviously a difference of kind, not of degree only, which I might perhaps best express by the word " pure." This pleasure is closely connected in my mind with an inward conviction that there is in me a tendency towards good, not unlike the attraction of plants towards light. And I find, by what others say and do, that my own experience in this respect is by no means exceptional, but that in different degrees it is so common as to be practically universal. I may, therefore, without exaggeration regard it as a law of human nature. Those who argue that goodness is merely a form of selfishness, as that word is commonly understood, seem to me to be mere theorists, and to shut out of sight one side of human nature, quite as much so as that erudite German philosopher who is said to have written a book to prove that all morality is a function of the digestive organs. I find, moreover, that this moral sense has a tendency to develope under favourable circumstances both in human history and in the individual. In other words, I see in the world an evident evolution of moral good.

"I turn to the physical world, and there I find a similar tendency—the gradual dying out of the weak and sickly, that the strong may survive and the race may become stronger. What the agriculturist and the horticulturist do artificially, Nature has been doing for herself for thousands upon thousands of years. And the climax of this process is man, who has been all along becoming as a whole more perfect in powers of thought, organisation, and moral capacity. There is between the highest civilised man and the primitive savage a difference almost as great as between the latter and the highest existing animal. The more I consider the facts, the more clearly it appears to me that the evolution in nature and in moral goodness are connected together, and are the results of one great principle inherent in all things. I am aware, of course, that such evolution in nature may be explained as the direct result of natural laws; but I cannot feel satisfied that these exclude the working of a higher agency behind them, though I honestly confess myself incapable of scientifically proving it.

"So much I learn from science and the ordinary experience of life; but can they tell me more? Can they account for this principle? Can they tell me whence it came? To what it finally tends? No. Science most emphatically claims only a knowledge of the 'how.' The original 'whence' and the ultimate 'whither' are beyond her ken. Still less have I learnt these from the ordinary experience of life. My own innate consciousness may have told me more, but being what I am, I cannot separate this altogether from what has come to me through my religious training. Now religion does claim to give me an answer. She refers this great natural and moral principle to a Being whom she calls God, and she seeks in various ways to define what God is. So far as she does this, she does not contradict science. It may be true that science knows no God, but it is equally true that she does not deny God. Science alone is agnostic no doubt, she is not atheistic.

"But then at this point I am confronted with a new difficulty. Different men, and men in different ages and in different countries, have found or accepted very divergent opinions about God. To speak of no more subtle distinctions, how am I to choose between polytheism, pantheism, monotheism? The mere fact that I have been brought up as a monotheist is not a sufficient reason for choosing the last; for on this ground a pagan savage would have just as good a reason for being a polytheist. I must decide the matter on other grounds.

"Polytheism is for me clearly out of the question. It is altogether too gross and anthropomorphic. It satisfies neither my thought nor my moral, nor my religious, feeling, and is in fact utterly repulsive. It is only where its distinctive features have been explained away as symbols, and it has been refined into something approaching very closely to monotheism or pantheism, that I can seriously look upon it as a religion at all. It is clearly a rudimentary stage through which races in their childhood pass, in their evolution of religious ideas and religious worship. Outwardly, it seems in most cases to have originated from a combination of ghost and nature-worship; inwardly, from a crude semi-religious fear of beings more powerful than men, which they tried to propitiate.

"I turn, therefore, to pantheism and monotheism. Which am I to choose? There is this difficulty at the outset, that though these terms can be so used as to express widely divergent views of God, yet, in fact, the religions and philosophies which are designated by them often approach very closely, and even shade off into, each other. The opinions which represent the farthest poles of either tendency may be rejected at once. I cannot believe God to be either, on the one hand, a pure abstraction or an automatic quasi-physical force, conceivably comparable to electricity. Nor, on the other hand, can I think of God as a humanlike being, a merely glorified man. The God I seek is neither neuter nor anthropomorphic. Nor, again, in choosing between pantheism and monotheism, am I much helped by what is, roughly speaking, called Natural religion. The natural religious tendency, as clearly seen by those who have thought out religion for themselves,—the Greeks, for example,— is from polytheism to pantheism. Indeed, in some cases, as especially in modern Germany, it seems to be from monotheism to pantheism. But in thinking the matter over, I am inclined to believe that this last change is a reaction from a popular semi-polytheistic and anthropomorphic, to a more philosophical, view of God. If so, it bears some analogy to the religious evolution of the ancient Greeks. And this makes me wonder whether, after all, there may not be truth on both sides. Personality, as generally understood, may be, from the philosophical point of view, a crude anthropomorphic conception of God. It does not help us, except by very imperfect analogies, to understand God's work in the physical world. But as a practical basis for religious faith, it seems truer to me than regarding God as a mere force. I want a God to love and revere, a God to depend upon as the source of good,—a God, in short, with character; but a force has no character."

I have thus roughly sketched the way in which I

can fancy an intelligent young man thinking out his religious doubts and difficulties. Nor have I cared to make any very clear distinction between what he may be presumed to have received by tradition, to have learnt by study, or to have thought out originally for himself. But I am supposing that he has made whatever he has received thoroughly his own, so that, in this sense, he is really thinking out his own thoughts. Now, what effect would the old evidential argument from prophecy have upon such a man? Would it do anything to convince him? Would it not rather disgust and repel him? Would he not certainly feel that the cause of Christianity must be very desperate if it needs arguments of this sort, like the drowning man who catches at a straw? But what would his attitude towards the Bible probably be? Without taking into account variation of sentiment, character, and circumstances which influence different individuals in different ways, would it not probably be something of this kind? The Old Testament as a whole might appear to him a curious mixture of confusing religious notions, somewhat hard moral sentiments, and dry religious annals, written from a single and apparently narrow point of view. And yet for all that he would probably have conceived, as he has read them or heard them, a vague liking for some special chapters which attracted him, partly by their beauty of language and partly by something which appealed half unconsciously to his better self. If so, is it not likely that, in such a state of mind as I have described, he would feel an interest in a serious study of the Old Testament? He would read it, of course, in a different way and in a different spirit to that in which he had read it before. He would, on the one hand, avail himself of the best information in various branches of Bible study; but, on the other hand, he would read it without prejudice in either direction, with the pure and honest desire to ascertain what Bible writers really said and meant, and what they may, or may not, have had to teach others. Surely such an one would be led to welcome the religion of the prophets and psalmists, as giving, on the whole, by far the most perfect and, as compared with other ancient literature, practically a unique, example of monotheism. In reading some of the early books of the Bible,—parts of Genesis and Exodus, for example,—he might be tempted to smile at their simple, childlike anthropomorphism; but he would soon discover that these mark but an early stage in the religious history of the Jews. As he passed on to a later period, he would find the conception of God becoming more and more spiritual, till it reaches its climax in such passages as Isa. lv. and Ps. cxxxix.

He might find a very instructive example of a transition between, or a combination of, those two views of God, the anthropomorphic and the spiritual (shewing how one grew out of the other), in the quaint story found in Ex. xxxiii. 12—xxxiv. 7. In v. 13, Moses prays Yahweh to shew him His ways. This being granted in v. 17, Moses further asks that He will shew him His glory. To this there is, as the narrative now stands, a double answer. Yahweh first promises that He will make His goodness pass before Moses, and proclaim the name of Yahweh as the God of mercy. But the second answer takes an almost entirely anthropomorphic form. Yahweh's face cannot be seen, not because it is a thing impossible in itself, but because it would involve the inevitable death of the beholder, just as a flash of lightning kills one with whom it comes in contact. But something will be done towards gratifying Moses' request. There is a rock near Yahweh, on which he is directed to stand. Yahweh will put him in a cleft of the rock, and cover him with His hand till He has passed by; then He will remove His hand, and Moses will be permitted to see His back. But when the event is actually described a few verses below (xxxiv. 5-7), the anthropomorphic conception of God again passes almost into the spiritual. "And Yahweh descended in the cloud, and stood with him there, and proclaimed the name of Yahweh. And Yahweh passed by before him, and proclaimed Yahweh, Yahweh, a God full of compassion and gracious, slow to anger and plenteous in mercy and truth: keeping mercy for thousands, forgiving iniquity and transgression and sin, and that will by no means clear the guilty," &c.[1]

The supposed student would also discover that

---

[1] It is a matter of considerable critical interest whether we should regard this whole passage as it now stands as a revised recension, according to new lights, of a primitive document, or as the work of a mind hovering between the old and new learning. But this is not a

the religion of the Jews underwent another change. There are significant hints that it was originally polytheistic, or at least contained polytheistic elements. The worship of the Teraphim, or images of household gods much like the Roman Penates, was common, at least up to the time of David. It is spoken of as a thing not at all surprising that there should be an image of this sort in David's house (1 Sam. xix. 13). It appears also that Yahweh was regarded as the God of the Jews much in the same way that Dagon was the God of the Philistines, or Chemosh was the God of the Moabites, or Molech the God of the Ammonites. The point of the story of the disaster to Dagon's image is not that it represented a false god, but that in the image falling down before the Ark, Dagon shewed, however unwillingly, his inferiority to Yahweh. The contest between the God of the Hebrews and the Gods of the Egyptians in the ten plagues points to the same idea. It was also not an uncommon belief that Yahweh had no power except in His own country. David complains to Saul that, in being chased from his fatherland, he was driven from the inheritance of Yahweh, and was thereby forced to serve other gods (1 Sam. xxvi. 19). Even at the time when the story of Jonah took a Jewish shape, it is thought not an unnatural, though an erroneous, belief on the prophet's part that he could escape from Yahweh's power by leaving his native country (Jonah i. 3).

question of very great theological importance. In any case it shews, better perhaps than any other passage of the Old Testament, how the higher view of God gradually supplanted the lower.

And so we can trace a gradual change from the thought of the inferiority of the heathen gods, as compared with the God of Israel, to that of the utter absurdity of worshipping nonentities, as we find it expressed, for example, in the great Captivity prophet. How could rational men worship gods which were so feeble that they could not even do harm? (Isa. xli. 23).

But even in this book the prevailing thought is the absurdity of representing a spiritual God in material forms at all. How the prophet laughs at the thought of the Babylonian gods, jostled together faces downward and carted off by the victors in ignominious triumph! (Isa. xlvi. 1-2) or of the image whose more useful counterpart has already served to the worshipper's creature comforts! "He burneth part thereof in the fire; with part thereof he eateth flesh; he roasteth roast, and is satisfied: yea, he warmeth himself, and saith, Aha, I am warm, I have seen the fire; and the residue thereof he maketh a god, even his graven image: he falleth down unto it, and worshippeth, and prayeth unto it, and saith, Deliver me; for thou art my god" (xliv. 16-17). This thought, again, was largely due to the influence of Deuteronomy, where the prohibition of idols is emphatically based on the fact that the Israelites saw no form of God in Horeb (Deut. iv. 12, 15, 16).

Above all, the supposed student of Scripture would be struck by the moral greatness of the God of Israel. The Yahweh of the prophets is the source of all righteousness, purity, and tenderness; and in common with this is the feeling that all immorality is an offence against God's holiness, and therefore requires His pardon. We accept such doctrines as a matter of course; but *then* they were new truths which the world had yet to learn. The Jews learnt them first, and they taught them to the world.

But even the Jews did not learn them all at once. The earlier belief about sacrifice was not so very unlike that of the Pagans. God delighted in sacrifices as such. He took a sort of human pleasure in them. He smelled the sweet savour of Noah's sacrifice, and was so pleased that He determined never again to curse the ground for man's sake (Gen. viii. 20-22). We are reminded of the delight which the Homeric gods took in the sacrifices of the Greek heroes. But how unlike this is to the language of Isa. i., or of Pss. l. and li. It is clear that both prophets and psalmists are contending against a false notion of sacrifice. Purity of heart and hand, thanksgiving, obedience, penitence, are the true sacrifices which God requires. It is quite true that after the Captivity we find the sacrifices not only restored, but developed into a new and complicated system. But their character is in a great measure changed. They have become object-lessons intended to enforce the very truths on which the prophets had been insisting. Even a sacrifice once offered, as it seems, to the heathen deity Azazel, is so transformed as to become a significant and very instructive feature in the ritual of the Great Day of Atonement (Lev. xvi. 8-10).[1]

Even at best the Jewish conception of God was not absolutely perfect. As in His nature, so also in His character, it contained anthropomorphic elements which it never seems to have thrown off completely. Sin was thought of still more or less as a personal affront to God, demanding His vengeance. It was quite a natural thing for God to be jealous of idolatry as an infringement of His rights. There is an almost childlike simplicity in those beautiful appeals which Moses and Joshua make to God's dignity not to allow His name to be dishonoured among the heathen (*e.g.* Ex. xxxii. 12, Josh. vii. 9). Thoughts like these colour even the later language of the Old Testament; unless we are to suppose that such words as wrath and jealousy had come, as with ourselves, to be merely figurative expressions for the hatred of wrong in itself. But this, like some other recognised imperfections in the elementary religion of Judaism, need form no stumbling-block to this earnest inquirer, for it would help to point the way to the more perfect teaching of Jesus Christ. But it is a matter of very great importance to realise that the religion which in its expanded Christian form is becoming the religion of the world, which is the only religion which inseparably connects theology and morality, the only religion which teaches a God such as to satisfy at

---

[1] It is a very significant fact that the word atonement only occurs twice in A.V. outside the Priestly Post-Captivity portions of the Hexateuch.

once the religious instinct and the requirements of thought, began with the Jews, and found some of its best exponents in the Jewish prophets.

Moreover, the student in question could not help being deeply impressed with the fact that these great Jewish teachers one after another claim unequivocally to be speaking the words of God. Without taking a too narrow and literal view of such an expression as "thus saith Yahweh," without forgetting the manifest limitations of prophetic knowledge and foresight, he could not help seeing that they honestly believed that they were God's special messengers to their people, and that their work it was to awaken a new and purified religious spirit, which was promised first to the Jews, and through them to all the world; and he would gladly recognise that the result in both cases has proved the fulfilment of the promise, even though not precisely in the way, nor as yet in the degree, in which they themselves expected.

If he once satisfied himself that these things were so, would he be likely to stop at this point? Would he not feel, as he studied the prophets with increasing earnestness and pleasure, that they were leading him towards a religion so purifying and so ennobling that it must be true? Would he not in all probability turn again with greater interest to the New Testament, and learn to see in its familiar words a new power stirring and directing his own spiritual life? It is needless to trace any further the possible religious history of such a man, except perhaps to ask whether he would not be far more likely after such an experience to live his Christianity out in deed and power. For he would have found in it an ideal compared with which neither science nor philosophy nor any mere religionism have anything to offer.

But it may be objected, "You have been supposing a very special case, a man possessed of remarkably high character and exceptional religious tastes. What about the pronounced infidel or the profligate, the man who openly denies God or professes contempt for all moral principles, and looks upon religion as an effete superstition? Would the study of the prophets have any effect on such a man?" Very possibly not. Such a state of mind shews a want both of culture and of natural endowment which must be dealt with by other means. At any rate, it is obvious that one who will not listen either to the voice of Christ, or to his own conscience, is hardly likely to study with patience or profit the teaching of the prophets. But, after all, it is not in these half-developed and one-sided characters that the great danger to our faith lies, but rather in that unconscious infidelity or half-faith of those who have never learnt to doubt, just because they have never known what it is in the best and fullest sense to believe. It is quite possible to lay the utmost stress on the matter of faith, and not attach half enough importance to its quality. It may be willingly admitted that the instance which I have supposed is undoubtedly favourable to my argument, but I do not think it is really so very exceptional.

Even if it were so, it may be fairly supposed that to one less favourably circumstanced by education and natural endowment, the study of the prophets is likely to have at least a proportionate value.

In fact the amount of influence exercised by prophecy in determining Christian faith must depend very largely upon the individual, and cannot be gauged by any theory of Christian Evidences. What we need, however, to realise is that Prophecy was an essential stage in that Great Revelation which began in distant ages and is not even yet complete, the work of Him, who is to lead men into all truth. But, if so, it is clear that a serious study of the Prophets may be a very real help in the building up of Christian faith and Christian character.

www.ingramcontent.com/pod-product-compliance
Lightning Source LLC
Chambersburg PA
CBHW020826230426
43666CB00007B/1122